Up from
Scapegoating

Up from Scapegoating

*Awakening Consciousness
in Groups*

Arthur D. Colman

Chiron Publications • Wilmette, Illinois

"Depth Consultation in Organizations: Awakening Collective Consciousness," Chapter 6, is based on the original by Arthur D. Colman, "Depth Consultation," in Murray Stein and John Hollwitz, eds., *Psyche at Work: Workplace Applications of Jungian Analytical Psychology,* Chiron Publications, 1992, pp. 92–117. Copyright © 1992 by Chiron Publications.

Library of Congress Catalog Card Number: 95–14098

Printed in the United States of America.
Copyedited by Siobhan Drummond.
Book design by Vivian Bradbury.
Cover design by D. J. Hyde.

Library of Congress Cataloging-in-Publication Data:

Colman, Arthur D., 1937–
    Up from scapegoating : awakening consciousness in groups / Arthur
D. Colman.
      p.   cm.
    Includes bibliographical references and index.
    ISBN 0–933029–95–0
    1. Group relations training.   2. Scapegoat—Psychological aspects.
3. Collective behavior.   I. Title.
HM134.C635 1995
302'.14—dc20   95–14098
                                               CIP

ISBN 0–933029–95–0

To the *A. K. Rice Institute* and its members,
the *C. G. Jung Institute of San Francisco* and its members,
and our individual and collective struggles
to awaken consciousness in our own organizations and beyond

Contents

Foreword

Up from Scapegoating: Awakening Consciousness in Groups rests on a very large vision. Collective consciousness is the human faculty least developed in our species and the one we need most to help restore the balance of life on our planet. Psychologists and environmentalists, to name but a few of those who attempt to bring awareness and change to our darkly troubled interspecies dance, will appreciate this book. It posits that by exploring the unfolding mythologies that live in groups and intergroups in a social system we can learn to speak a new language, one inclusive of both the individual and the group voice. To simultaneously hold meaning and purpose at both the individual and the group level of discourse is difficult; we particularly resist giving the group level awareness its due, as if individual identities and connections would then be obliterated. But surely we need such an inclusive language. Arthur Colman's book leads us toward it.

This book is a significant contribution in a field of study which is both relatively new and poorly articulated because of our biases and its complexity. Many have worked to enhance our knowledge of group phenomena, but few have focused on its depth dimension: none, in my estimate, have managed to embrace it and articulate it so comprehensively. Arthur clearly loves group relations work; his professional and personal life have been influenced and enriched by it. In turn he has been a major force in the field since its inception. His biographical sketch in the introduction attests to his participation, but it is most evident in the experimental truths which resonate throughout the text.

Arthur is a training analyst at the C. G. Jung Institute in San Francisco, and what is particularly new and intriguing here is the

Jungian orientation which flows through Arthur's writings. The group archetype described in this book now take its place with archetypes of similar dynamic flavor such as shadow, syzygy, ego, and Self. Formulating such an archetypal dimension not only integrates group relations theory with Jungian thought but also gives depth to the former and a badly needed home to group phenomena in the Jungian framework.

This latter conceptualization is long overdue. The Platonic tradition on which analytical psychology rests is most syntonic with what we observe of group life. Unlike most psychologies, the Jungian perspective sees the human being as a function of the psyche, and human events as translations of the elemental language of the psyche. That is, we are embedded in the unconscious and not the other way around. What is "inside" and "outside" becomes a point of view rather than a location. The notion of the ego as the ruling principle is put aside, and the ego is made subservient to the greater forces of the Self, however manifest. The Self is postulated to be the central organizing principle of the psyche—individual, group, society—and its structure defined in terms of the many archetypal forms that make up the collective unconscious. Consciousness by definition splits reality into polarities, but the view from the Self embraces the primordial oneness of existence.

The goal of individual analytic work is the development of a harmonious dialogue between the ego as the center of individual consciousness and the unconscious in whatever form it may manifest. The point is not to have a bigger and better ego but to mature the ego sufficiently so it will stand in relation and discourse with the archetypal energies of the Self. In parallel fashion, the individual members of a group are faced with the onslaught of unconscious dynamics that threaten to obliterate them or inflate them beyond recognition. Group members must learn to identify and relate to these energies in a constructive manner. However, paradoxically, that goal seems best actualized when viewing the experience from the group-as-a-whole perspective, where the individual is seen to be playing one of the many roles the group uses to express the patterns ignited by its life force. Arthur elaborates this phenomenon in his chapter "Jung's Concept of Individuation and the Scapegoat." Here, evil comes alive as we become frighteningly aware of the tendency in groups to experience their wholeness by unconsciously rejecting an undesired part as their scapegoat.

Jung's system is empirically grounded but also very complex because it has evolved from a monumental study of religions throughout the world and across time. Its aesthetic potential is overshadowed by its religious focus, but that too is there to be witnessed. As his theory states, the archetypes cannot be known directly but their energies show up as images. An evolving group seen from the vantage point of its imaginal underpinnings is a truly magnificent spectacle. The quality of its voice resounds more and more beautifully as it moves from its "monkey mind" stage to the entrainment of its various parts toward the creation of a mythological operatic drama in various stages or in one glorious finale. My favorite consulting work is with large groups because they most fully embody and deliver this level of experience. Therefore, Arthur's chapters 4 and 5, "Exploring the Group Mystery: The Organ of Group Consciousness" and "The Language of the Group: Stories, Myths, and Archetypes," respectively, speak to me most vividly.

A consultation Arthur and I did in Moscow in August 1991 with a large group at a conference called "Dreaming in Russia" best exemplified for me the music that groups create as they explore their complex inner patterns. We worked with multinational and multilingual members, so when the community congregated, interpreters were a necessity. The first group meetings were laboriously self-conscious as every sentence was translated into several languages. However, by the end of the ten days of the conference, the large group had the quality of a high mass or Gregorian chant in multiple tongues. We had learned how to listen and find patterns of meaning in what had been a cacophony of sounds.

That conference, organized and directed by Boston-based Robert Bosnak and his Russian colleague Karen Melik-Simonian, served as a rare example of a consultation with a large group at a time and place of cataclysmic political, economic, and ideological transition. Periods of crossings in individual and social systems are characterized by extremely rich, often horrific, and always dangerously absorbing imagery erupting from the death and rebirth archetype energized. This particular event took place outside Moscow during the 1991 coup that finally ended seventy years of communism and Soviet rule. We could all glimpse the newly emerging mythological forms embodied in the psyches of participant Russians, Lithuanians, Armenians, and others as the large group progressed through its own death phase into symbols heralding the rebirth potential. These visions in our group could not fully coalesce; the countries represented at the conference are still bleeding today. However, what we did see in its most articulated form was the phenomenon of mirroring. In the microcosm of this large group were reflected the death-dealing transformative patterns ongoing in the larger culture. Although actual communication lines between us and the rest of Russia and the world had largely broken down, we were functioning at such a profound level of unconscious activation—so deep within the realm of the Self and its overriding unifying collective energies—that our large group innocently and simultaneously enacted the ongoing national dramas as they happened.

Another major advantage to viewing groups from the perspectives of the Self, related to that which Arthur explores in chapter 6, comes from one of Jung's most creative contributions. He was the only psychologist to suggest that drives are both instinctual and spiritual and to introduce the dimension of the sacred. Clearly, it was the image of God in the human psyche and not God per se that he studied. He referred to the central energy of the Self as that meaning which held the highest value for the individual. I have observed that if at the appropriate moment a group is alerted to this force—right as it happens—members are less likely to reject an interpretation, instead becoming receptive to an image that allows the central dynamic to emerge. The group is then moved forward as if by magic to a more egalitarian, inclusive, and satisfying resolution of conflict and sustainable definition of purpose and goals. This ideal may not always be actualized, for groups are quite varied and complex; it takes much training and sensitivity to be able to intervene at the right time and to hold the dynamic power of the moment. But when such intervention works, hope is renewed for the successful development of collective consciousness in humankind.

The philosophical underpinnings of Jungian thought and its marriage with group relations theory contribute to the foundation of Arthur's formulations on groups but hardly delimit creative leaps displayed in the narrative. As we travel the pages of

his book we link minds with shamanism as well as other medita-
tive traditions and theoretical perspectives, and we explore with
him the origin, development, and language of the group archetype and the applications of this knowledge as consultant to
diverse social systems. Most compelling in his writing is the
strongly personal quality of his communication, which grounds
the very abstract conceptual frame that has evolved from his
immediate experience. His highly developed aesthetic faculty
and sense of humor emerge in the choice and scope of example
and illustration as well as in his writing style.

Arthur and I have collaborated for twenty years consulting
and conceptualizing our work with groups. It is with great pride
and pleasure that I write the foreword and so participate in
launching this book.

—Pilar Montero

Pilar Montero, Ph.D., is a Jungian analyst and consultant in group
relations.

Introduction

One "royal road to the unconscious" is dreams. Another is collective experience. In my work with groups, particularly large groups, I often feel as if I am in the middle of a dream, a very large, numinous, and often incomprehensible dream, and it was the power of the archetypal group dream that first led me to explore Jung's psychology. One of Jung's great discoveries was the reality of the collective unconscious, the presence of the unconscious in the collective and the collective in the unconscious. I have found no other framework that better explains the mythic cornucopia of group life. Freud's view of groups was brilliant but too limited—a theory based on one myth of a horde of brothers struggling with the wish to devour their father (Freud 1921, pp. 69–143). Sociological work on groups too often leaves out both the unconscious and the mystery.

Wilfred Bion's *Experiences in Groups* (1959), particularly his elaboration of "group mind" and "basic assumptions," is extremely valuable; but like Freud's theories, his ideas do not encompass the mythic largess that infuses group experience. Jung rescued me. His archetypal world of the collective unconscious was rich enough to give meaning to all that I experienced in the world of groups. Unfortunately, Jung had little to say about the innards of group life; his "collective" was abstracted from the real-time process, perhaps because of his profound mistrust of the collective made manifest in flesh-and-blood human groups (Jung 1921, par. 761). Nevertheless, Jung's psychology, with concepts like the collective unconscious and its focus on archetype and myth, has much to offer this field. Analytic psychology has begun recently to explore group phenomena with some intensity (Stein and Hollwitz 1992).

In this volume I am interested in using Jungian and related depth psychology concepts to explore the nature of the boundary between the individual and the group, without assuming that the individual or individual consciousness is in center stage. I am interested in exploring the concept of a group archetype and group complex as fundamental to child and adult development as the ego, shadow, or parental archetypes and complexes. I am interested in exploring consciousness and the unconscious as both individual and group states, entertaining the idea that individuation is relevant to groups as well as to individuals and that the critical relationship between these two processes is manifested in the archetype of the scapegoat. I apply the concept of a group consciousness to group and organizational consultation and to the development of consciousness in infants and children. My approach is consonant with an ecological perspective, one in which the individual is no longer king and queen of the universe or even of the human species, one in which we (individual or group) are embedded in the world and it is embedded in us.

My professional interest in groups began early in my psychiatric residency training at the University of California, San Francisco, in 1963. Psychiatry was then in transition from an individual-based psychoanalytic perspective, which had been in ascendance for more than two decades, to a more community-based view. (Psychopharmacology and brain research, the current frontrunners in psychiatry, were still dark horses.) San Francisco was a hotbed of interest for group and systems theory and method. Our teachers included Eric Berne and Fritz Perls, who used group settings to develop game and gestalt theory, respectively, Don Jackson and Virginia Satir, who developed much of modern family theory and therapy, and Maxwell Jones and Harry Wilmer, who pioneered milieu therapy on psychiatric wards. With such a formidable and charismatic array of teachers, it is no wonder that group, family, milieu, and systems therapy approaches joined individual therapy as cornerstones of my training.

My familiarity with group methods and theory provided an unexpected reward by keeping me in Washington during the Vietnam War. I was drafted into the Army in 1966 at a time when all physicians were typically assigned to Southeast Asia for a year or more. However, a psychiatrist was needed to run an experimental ward at Walter Reed Army Institute of Research, and

David Rioch, then the influential head of psychiatric research there and himself a Sullivanian psychoanalyst, was looking for an Army psychiatrist who knew something more than the individual psychoanalytic approaches. After a grueling six-hour interview, Rioch became convinced of my interest in groups and hired me with a guarantee that I would stay out of Vietnam. One of Rioch's life missions, which influenced me greatly, was his commitment to increase our psychological knowledge about group life so that its conflicts would not need to be acted out through war. Unlike Jung, who believed that the salvation of our species could only come through increased consciousness in the individual, Rioch, guided mainly by his experience consulting to political and military leadership, saw the group, not the individual, as the unit of consciousness with the most leverage on human survival.

Rioch thought highly of group relations conferences and introduced me to Ken Rice and Wilfred Bion, group relations theory's creators. At these conferences I learned a method for exploring the group and institutional unconscious *in situ* (Miller and Rice 1965). Later, Jung's archetypal approach added theoretical depth to this method, and Pilar Montero and I were able to incorporate these ideas in explanatory workshops that provide a perspective for entering the world of the group unconscious that parallels the way analysts enter the unconscious of their analytic patients. This perspective provides one of two experiential and practical frameworks for my work with groups and the essays of this book.

The other perspective is traditional and modern shamanism. In order to consult to a group in depth, one must enter another world, a world no longer centered in one's own individual consciousness or personal unconscious. The consultant becomes part of the group consciousness itself, retaining only enough individual observing ego to be able to give words to the emotions, images, and myths of that collective experience. This ability to let go of one's individual consciousness, to give oneself almost completely over to another reality, requires trust in the existence of that other reality, the "other world." Without such trust there is no crossing over the boundary from one consciousness to another, any more than one can be psychologically reborn if one is afraid to die.

Consulting to a group through entering its consciousness is

a little like taking a rowboat across a river obscured by deep fog. Fear and common sense both suggest caution, perhaps waiting until the fog clears and there is a good view of the other side. The shamanic perspective is a valuable model to interpose here, for the shaman's competence is entering the "other world" in order to envision and heal. The shamanic initiation involves years of personal ordeal to develop sufficient trust in the value of this crossing to outweigh the fear of the "other side," or in modern psychological language, the unconscious. Faced with the rowboat, the shaman might say, "Go now. Trust that there is another shore and a reason to cross. Oh, and don't bother to tie up the boat after you cross. Trust too that there will be a way back, a different way. In the healing of others, you too will heal. If the journey is worth taking, you too will change. No one who has really crossed over ever returns the same."

Consulting to a group is not unlike the shaman's healing journey at the behest of his or her patient and community, including the ever-present risks of inflation and overidentification. The consultant learns to travel in the group unconscious without losing sight of the task. But the dangers implicit to the consultant are evident to any citizen of a country in the midst of revolution, in the grip of racism, in the power of the scapegoat archetype. Jung's warning about the dangers of falling under the regressive pull of mass humanity should be heeded where possible. But most of us do not have the Alps and a tradition of neutrality to help protect us from the mob and its projecting dynamics; ultimately none of us can escape the web of group life. We are a sentient species and, as I suggest in the essay on development, individual consciousness is borne out of collective consciousness. We all carry a "group in the mind" within us. This is our heritage as a member of our species, from which there is no permanent protection except, perhaps, knowledge and more consciousness of our dual individual and group identities. We can, for example, pay more attention to the group archetypes that confront us in our living situations, to the kinds of authority we give to our leaders, and to the potential for learning and growth and healing that these powerful group forces carry.

Jung has often been called a shaman, and there is much that his methodology shares with the shamanic perspective. For Jung, the purpose of exploring the unconscious is to heal—self and other. The shamanic is also a healing perspective. For both Jung and the traditional shaman, healing occurs predominantly in the "other world," whether it is called the unconscious or the land of ancestors. But one important difference between the traditional shaman and modern therapists, from Jungian and most other models, is the role of the group both as an object of healing and in the healing process itself. For the shaman, healing is rarely a one-on-one encounter. The community is an integral part of the healing ceremony, and what the shaman finds when he or she crosses over into the other world may relate to individual, family, or community, or even to another part of the spirit world or cosmos. Unlike the modern therapist, the shaman is often called upon to heal the community or part of the community. This is because of the shamanic belief in a holistic perspective, in which distinctions between group and individual, humans and other animals, or even animate and inanimate, are not precise, particularly within the "other world" where healing occurs.

Of course, Jung was no stranger to this point of view, as his wide-ranging interpretations of his own and others' dreams suggests. His knowledge and ability to tap the collective unconscious and speak its meanings is legendary. I hope that the essays in this book can contribute to that part of Jung's legacy and to Rioch's connection between war and unconscious group process. Hopefully it will be useful in extending depth psychology's perspective to the problems of groups, institutions, and political systems.

1

Jung's Concept of Individuation and the Scapegoat

I HOLD THE JUNGIAN COMMUNITY, PARTICULARLY THE PART OF IT I know best, the C. G. Jung Institute of San Francisco, in extremely high regard. The institute is an intellectual and spiritual collective which has, over the past quarter century, helped its members and candidates develop as analysts, teachers, and individuals. But there have also been a number of casualties. One of these was a man who contracted AIDS and died. Despite his central teaching and analytic role in the institute, he kept his illness a virtual secret within the community. Consequently, the institute was unable to help him with his agonizing personal and professional troubles; we were also unable to provide desperately needed help for his clients, including the candidates he analyzed and supervised until the very last weeks. On other occasions several analysts have suffered with sexual ethical problems with their patients, resulting in psychic damage on both sides. Again the Jungian community was used less as a resource for healing and more as a judgmental group after the fact.

In the course of psychological work in the institute necessitated by these tragedies—again, after the fact—it became clearer and clearer that one of the critical reasons why these individuals were unable to use the community for help, why we couldn't or wouldn't serve their needs, was because they served ours. In some

1

horrible unconscious way these valuable and much loved colleagues, some of the most creative people in our institute, were also our collective shadow and our scapegoats. They acted for us, saving us from our own fantasies and impulses. To really be of use to them, we would have had to acknowledge their perverse role in our lives. It took a personal and professional catastrophe to bring the group's role in their problems (and theirs in ours) into consciousness. For reasons of propriety and confidentiality, I do not plan to analyze these particular circumstances further. But they form the emotional basis of some of the concepts I will present.

My interest here is in the group's role in individuation and, conversely, the role of individuation in group life. I will focus on one critical intersection between the individuation process and group life, on the archetypal creature known as the scapegoat.

To begin with, individuation is defined by Jung as "The development of the psychological individual as a being, distinct from the general collective psychology. Individuation, therefore, is a process of differentiation, having for its goal the development of the individual personality" (1921, par. 757).

Jung devotes much of his later work to fleshing out this definition, particularly in chronicling the various paths that humans have walked in order to search for their spiritual centers.

In the most general sense, Jung's definition establishes a polarity between the process of individuation and the requirements of the group. But he also sees each person requiring a close and intense relationship with group life, what he calls a "collective relationship." He considers this to be an initiation into the psychological world of adaptation, a preliminary accomplishment necessary to the more complex goal of individuation. Thus he states:

> Under no circumstances can individuation be the sole aim of
> psychological education. Before it can be taken as a goal, the
> educational aim of adaptation, to the necessary minimum of
> collective norms, must first be attained. If a plant is to unfold
> its specific nature to the full, it must first be able to grow in
> the soil in which it is planted. (Ibid., par. 760)

As Jung described it, an individual at the beginning of the individuation process feels suspended between two ways of being in the world. A part of him or her is still invested in dependency, continuing to cleave to hard-earned comforts, commitment to society's rules and regulations, and valued memberships in particular subgroups. At the same time, there is the beginning of a powerful urge to disengage with many of society's norms and instead be directed by a newly emerging inner authority. Jung adds:

> Individuation is always, to some extent, opposed to collective norms. It means separation and differentiation from the general, and a building of the particular—not a particular that is sought out, but one that is already ingrained in the psychic constitution. (Ibid., par. 761)

Jung saw the individuation process as a long and mostly solitary affair, although the dyad in the form of a helpful, sensitive person (such as therapist, lover, or friend) may play an important role. However, in discussing a similar facilitating role for the group in the individuation process, Jung is at his most acerbic.

> To experience transformation in the group and to experience it in oneself are two totally different things. A group experience takes place on a lower level of consciousness than the experience of an individual. If it is a very large group, the collective psyche will be more like the psyche of an animal, which is the reason why the ethical attitude of large organizations is always doubtful. If, therefore, I have a so-called collective experience as a member of a group, it takes place on a lower level of consciousness than if I had the experience myself, alone. (1950, par. 225)

In a more tolerant vein, Jung adds:

> The group can give the individual a courage, a bearing, and a dignity that may easily get lost in isolation. It can awaken within him the memory of being a man among men. But that does not prevent something else from being added, which he may not possess as an individual. Such unearned gifts may seem a special favor of the moment, but in the long run there is a danger of the gift becoming a loss, since human nature has a weak habit of taking gifts for granted. (Ibid., par. 228)

In his later writings Jung holds out more hope that the tension between the images and values of the group and those of one's unique individuality can be resolved eventually. He suggests that once the individual is aware enough of his or her own nature and the threat from the collective decreases, then each part can nurture the other. John Perry, in his book *The Heart of History* (1987), points out that even though Jung in some later seminars did deal with the role of service to the community in individuation, modern analysts usually give short shrift to this element of the individuation process.

Jung held to his mostly negative convictions about groups even when the survival of his own work was at stake. Unlike Freud, who was far more comfortable with and tolerant toward the vicissitudes of group life and who saw his ideas integrally involved with the promulgation of analytic institutes, Jung did not allow an institute to bear his name or espouse his theory until almost on his death bed. According to Joseph Wheelwright, an analyst who went to him in Zurich with the mission of beginning the first Jungian institute in the United States in San Francisco, Jung demurred until the very end before finally yielding to the pressure. His apocryphal utterance is often quoted in the halls of the San Francisco institute:

> Make it disorganized, this group of yours. Make the new Institute as disorganized as possible. Anything organized will kill us entirely.

Recent evidence suggests that Jung's views on the formation of the San Francisco institute and other institutes, including the one in Zurich, were actually quite specific. Wheelwright's interpretation captured a pervasive spirit in Jungian psychology; not only does the utterance continue to be quoted, but the institute in San Francisco has consciously tried to live up to it. The committee and authority structures have always been diffuse and confusing, mitigating against any decision being made smoothly or quickly. Yet we pride ourselves on the way the institute has nurtured the individuation process of candidate members, administrators, and associated lay people. Until recently we have had an almost phobic attitude toward trying to understand our own unconscious group process. But it has now become generally accepted that this lack of attention has taken its toll and created victims.

Understanding our own unconscious group process is a phenomenon which needs to be reevaluated. For example, in what circumstances will understanding the unconscious aspects of group life make a difference in the individual's ability to deal defensively with the negative group forces that Jung so feared? Or, from a more positive angle, could understanding more about these forces allow a facilitating and creative relationship to develop between the individuating person and his or her important groups?

In answering these questions which relate individuation and the group unconscious, we must first encounter the archetype of the scapegoat. This juxtaposition is less unlikely when one considers the usual fate of our spiritual heroes, ancient and modern. It is not enough to blame the culture, as we often do, for example, when we say that the world wasn't ready for Jesus, for Martin Luther King Jr., for Gandhi, for Anwar Sadat. Instead we must try to understand the process.

Following Jung, we know that individuation always necessitates the individual challenging the group and its norms in order to fashion one's own ethical framework, in order to be true to oneself. But there is no such thing as a painless or safe way to deny the group. There are always profound consequences to the individual, for groups as entities do not take kindly to such defections from their ranks; defectors threaten its cohesion and unity. If the defection is significant enough, the group will defend itself by invoking the scapegoating dynamic. Or, put another way, groups, like individuals, are always in pursuit of wholeness, and, like individuals who reject shadow elements of themselves by projecting them out onto the environment, the group will create victims—scapegoats—rather than accommodate diversity within its corpus. Thus the individual seeking his or her own way must face the prospect of becoming a scapegoat just as the group may need to find a scapegoat in order to deal with tension and the threat of fragmentation and disintegration. These two often asynchronous processes make for a complicated web of interactions and meanings which needs to be explored event by event. One important implication, however, is that the question of who really is being served in a given psychological event, individual or group, both or neither, is always open and must always be carefully explored.

These observations about individuation and scapegoating are not simply abstractions; they can be critical in clinical assessment as well as in other social and political situations. For example, one woman, call her Victoria, typical of many others, left husband, family, and home after reading Betty Friedan's *The Feminine Mystique* (1963) and joined a women's group. She felt she was attending to her own inner calling in making these changes in her life. But she was also in some ways a creation of the feminist movement and, more specifically, of the needs of the other members of the women's group to have at least one of their ranks act out all their wishes for heroic independence. The other group members stayed close to home and the marital bed while glorying vicariously in Victoria's courage. But Victoria had little inside of her to match their projections—she tumbled to the edge of sanity and suicide, more a scapegoat of the women's movement and her women's group than an individuating heroine. Similarly, many young men have gone off to war in what they experience as their own heroic quest, but they are really scapegoats of the frustrated power urges and waning sexuality of their middle-aged fathers who rule family and country.

I do not mean to imply that these and many other similar examples are either-or phenomena. The woman who leaves her family may be living out her needs and so may the young men who go off to war, but the strength of the role that these individuals play for some group unconscious can make a decided difference in the outcome of what they view as their individual quests. Good clinicians should always address these distinctions, especially in the beginning of treatment. Part of therapeutic work is to help the patient become clear about what he or she is working out for others as well as themselves. Not to do so, to assume that individuals are acting out their inner psyche's urge alone, is to court disaster for patients. Furthermore, therapists may themselves use patients to serve their inner and outer needs for an "individuating" client, thereby scapegoating their patients to a therapeutic ethos of individuation and individualism.

The *Webster's College Dictionary* defines *scapegoat* as "a person or group made to bear the blame for others or to suffer in their place." The Bible offers a more active description:

> And Aaron shall lay both his hands upon the head of the live
> goat, and confess over him all the iniquities of the children
> of Israel, and all their transgressions in all their sins, putting
> them upon the head of the goat, and shall send him away by
> the hand of a fit man into the wilderness. (Lev. 16:21 KJV)

The following quote from a political science book illustrates
these definitions in a chilling way.

> In January 1970, Harold Wilson, then Prime Minister of
> England, Walter Annenburg, then American ambassador to
> the court of St. James, and C. Clyde Ferguson, the ex-dean of
> Howard University Law School, talked together about the
> fate of international relief during the war between Nigeria
> and Biafra. "If," Wilson said, with nods from his colleagues,
> "a million Ibos tribesmen have to die to preserve the unity of
> Nigeria, well, that is not too high a price to pay." (Jacob
> 1987, p. 261)

Unity is the important concept in all scapegoating activity;
the scapegoat represents the group's push toward its own wholeness by excluding its disparate elements. Thus scapegoating can
be detected anywhere there is a transfer of negative attribution
from one part of the system to another, or from one part of the
system to an object outside the system, in order to fulfill what is
perceived to be a unifying survival function for the system as a
whole. The creation of a scapegoat requires a process akin to the
psychological mechanisms of projection and projective identification in that it uses an other to contain aspects of oneself.

The scapegoat is created by "projecting" the darker side of
group life, the darker side being the reality of evil and sin in society. For the individual, the shadow contains those elements of the
psyche that are not accepted as his or her own. As individuals we
attempt to project that shadow onto others. Likewise, the group
finds common negative ground in the scapegoat. But the scapegoat is not identical to the shadow; the scapegoat is a collective
creation, a symbolic compromise for many individuals' negative
projections. One can say that the scapegoat is humanity's societal
vessel for the shadow—a vessel which is, by definition, innocent
of the burden it assumes.

The scapegoat is a very ancient archetype and scapegoating

7

an ancient activity, so ancient that there are few primitive societies where evidence of the practice has not been found.[1] We have records of animals used as scapegoats that go back to ancient Hittite and Sanskrit texts. The works of modern authors who have used the scapegoat as a major theme (Dostoyevsky, Jackson, Lessing, for example) all hearken back to ancient days and a collective symbol that incorporates the worst of our projections in a strange, inanimate object. It is an image that taps our most primitive parts even today. An early biblical story, the basis of Yom Kippur and one that underlies the crucifixion of Jesus captures the fundamental Western image of the scapegoat.

The story begins with the Israelites fleeing Egypt. Aaron and God soon find that the law and monotheism are not sufficient to contain the Israelites who, after years of enforced slavery, have no experience taking responsibility for their own behavior. The priests are overwhelmed with the sin offerings of a guilty people and begin a return to primitive practices rather than staying within the new laws. After several priests have been killed for violating the law, God takes a new look at what is really possible with his chosen people. First the priests create a Day of Atonement, the current Jewish holiday of Yom Kippur, during which individual and collective sins of omission and commission are acknowledged and forgiven. But even this symbolic process is not sufficient, and the scapegoat is added.

> But the goat, on which the lot fell to be the scapegoat, shall
> be presented alive before the Lord, to make an atonement
> with him, and to let him go for a scapegoat into the wilderness. (Lev. 16:10)

The power of this biblical scapegoating process is seen in the phenomena of contagion. Referring to the man who takes the scapegoat into the wilderness, the narrative reads:

> And he that let go the goat for the scapegoat shall wash his
> clothes, and bathe his flesh in water, and afterward come
> into the camp. (Lev. 16:26)

The process of contagion underlines a frequent functional difference between group projection and the creation of the scapegoat and individual projection and the creation of the external bad object. In scapegoating, the projection is so generalized that there is little possibility of retrieval. A boundary is erected between group members and scapegoat—the wilderness or death itself—which insures what Hitler called "the final solution." Contagion requires this boundary. It is usually not enough for the scapegoat to be exiled. It must be destroyed. Even so, the symbolic vessel of the chosen animal cannot, because of its compromise quality, entirely contain the projected evil. The person who touches the scapegoat runs the risk of becoming the next scapegoat. Most horribly, the inadequacy of this process of containment gradually requires more and more potent symbols: objects or animals become increasingly inadequate and the flesh-and-blood scapegoating of humans and human subgroups becomes an acceptable practice.

This has required sophisticated rationalizations based on what Eric Erickson (1972) has called pseudospeciation to describe how a ruling or dominant group can justify locating the scapegoat function in its slaves or any other group cast as different and lower than itself. We have many examples from modern times—Armenians, Amerindians, South African Blacks, European Jews, Palestinians—all used as scapegoats in order to serve the hoped-for but specious unity of nationhood, much as individuals use shadow projections to serve the hoped-for but specious individuation of the person. And here we see a critical connection between the growth processes in individuals and in groups, for scapegoats not only deter group development but also hamper integration of shadow projections, a necessary step in the individuation process. As long as there are scapegoats—unintegrated shadow figures for the group—integration of the shadow within the individual is an illusion. One might even say that, for the individual, the process of individuation will always be held hostage to the presence of the scapegoat in the larger community.

Perhaps this feels like too heavy a burden for the individual to accept—to take on the responsibility for the scapegoats of the world as part and parcel of one's own attempts to integrate the personal shadow. Religious traditions have encountered this dilemma in the personage of Torquemada and the Spanish Inquisition, for example, and in the modern-day "neutrality" of the Pope and other religious leaders during the Holocaust. As we have seen, Jung's definition of individuation does not emphasize this connection between individual shadow and group scapegoat. His model, including the way it has been interpreted, tends to deemphasize the need to burden ourselves with the suffering of others as part of our own growth processes. To imagine the individuation process this way, however, is to accept that man is an island, that the suffering in the world is someone else's responsibility and does not grow from us or affect us. I for one reject this possibility. Individuation is an awesome burden precisely because it requires a connected, integrated outlook. Individuation demands that our bonds with other humans be included in the equation of our own development. We are all part of the scapegoating process. We are all a part of others' suffering. By our silence we give it passive support and supply our shadows with more energy, defeating each of our attempts at integrating the archetype. We must not only accept our responsibility for the scapegoat, we must do something about it. Individuation under any other terms can be just narcissistic play.

This does not mean that we should plunge into group life and good causes as an escape from the difficult aspects of our own individual work. Timing is critical. Group involvement can endanger individual development just as inappropriate family involvement or even analysis can be a dangerous intrusion or encumbrance. My point here is that because of the organic connection between shadow and scapegoat, group involvement is an unavoidable crossroad on the individuation path. As things go in matters of the unconscious, the more one tries to get away from the group issue, the more power it will gain, as Jung discovered in his painful failed dealings with the Nazis (Maidenbaum and Martin 1991).

There is a danger in meddling with an entrenched scapegoating system, namely, the risk of becoming a scapegoat oneself. And yet, silence in the face of such knowledge risks pseudoindividuation—an Eichmann-like irresponsibility which surely jeopardizes all subsequent attempts at personal development.

I want to use Ursula K. Le Guin's story entitled "The Ones Who Walk Away from Omelas" (1975) to explore and amplify some of the abstract themes of the scapegoat and individuation I have discussed above. The story draws its inspiration from William

10

James's view of the scapegoat in politics, the way nations develop victims in order to maintain a good life. Commenting on this, James says:

> Or if the hypothesis were offered us of a world in which . . . utopias should all be outdone, and millions kept permanently happy on the one simple condition that a certain lost soul on the far-off edge of things should lead a life of lonely torment, what except a specific and independent sort of emotion can it be which would make us immediately feel, even though an impulse arose within us to clutch at the happiness so offered, how hideous a thing would be its enjoyment when deliberately accepted as the fruit of such a bargain? (Le Guin 1975, p. 224)

It is this paradox of happiness with the scapegoat and unhappiness without that inspired Ursula K. Le Guin's modern parable.

To highlight James's question, Le Guin creates the community of Omelas, a beautiful, complex, and culturally rich utopia full of "mature, intelligent, passionate adults whose lives were not wretched. . . . The people of Omelas are happy people. Happiness is based on a just discrimination of what is necessary, what is neither necessary nor destructive, and what is destructive" (ibid., p. 226).[2] The people of Omelas decide on technology, on drugs, on religion, on personal and sexual relationship without guilt, all with "the sense of victory, surely, the celebration of courage" (ibid., p. 228).

Her description of Omelas is truly luscious. It is the quintessential postmodern utopian community, a developed, humanistic society containing many paradoxes and differences, and yet, as one reads one knows that something is missing. At one point she says to her reading audience: "Do you believe? Do you accept the city, the joy? No? Then let me describe one more thing." She goes on to tell about one hidden corner of Omelas where there is a dungeon, a foul-smelling cell with no window and little light. In it, there sits a child in abysmal and unending suffering. Le Guin describes it thus:

> It is feeble-minded. Perhaps it was born defective, or perhaps it has become imbecile through fear, malnutrition, and neglect. It picks its nose and occasionally fumbles vaguely

with its toes or genitals, as it sits hunched in the corner . . . .
Its buttocks and thighs are a mass of festered sores, as it sits
in its own excrement continually. (Ibid., p. 229)

Here we have the scapegoat, the counterbalance to the joy
of Omelas. Le Guin describes how all the people of Omelas know
about the scapegoat child but visit it infrequently. Still, so that the
children of Omelas will learn of its existence and *raison d'etre*,
Omelas has instituted a ritual time once a year during which all
the children who have reached a certain age and "seem capable
of understanding" must visit the child, mourn for the child, rage
for the child, and finally accept the child and its function for
them, for it is perfectly clear to the adults of Omelas that the
scapegoat is providing something critical for the community. Le
Guin tells us that the children do come to understand that "their
happiness, the beauty of their city, the tenderness of their friend-
ships," the health of their community rests on the poor child's
abysmal misery. The terms are clear to everyone. To accept the
scapegoat back into their society would mean the loss of all happiness (ibid.).

Le Guin's paradise, a metaphor for so many of our modern
paradises of the developed world, is based on the unhappiness of
an other, an innocent helpless child. As in the Bible story of the
scapegoat, there is nothing covert here and no question of relative guilt or innocence of the unhappy chosen one. The scapegoat child is innocent, and it is imprisoned through no fault of its
own. It exists with no other justification than keeping the people
happy.

Now do you believe in Omelas? the author asks.

Are they not more credible? But there is one more thing to
tell, and this is quite incredible.

At times one of the adolescent girls or boys who go to see
the child does not go home to weep or rage, does not, in
fact, go home at all. Sometimes also a man or woman much
older falls silent for a day or two, and then leaves home.
These people go out into the street, and walk down the street
alone. They keep walking, and walk straight out of the city of
Omelas, through the beautiful gates. They keep walking
across the farmlands of Omelas. Each one goes alone, youth
or girl, man or woman. Night falls; the traveler must pass

down village streets, between the houses with yellow-lit windows, and on out into the darkness of the fields. Each alone, they go west or north, towards the mountains. They go on. They leave Omelas, they walk ahead into the darkness, and they do not come back. The place they go towards is a place even less imaginable to most of us than the city of happiness. I cannot describe it at all. It is possible that it does not exist. But they seem to know where they are going, the ones who walk away from Omelas. (Ibid., p. 231)

The Omelas story, a modern fairy tale, is a variety of the traditional scapegoat scenario. From one perspective, the story could be profitably analyzed as representing various parts of the individual psyche and its pressure toward integration. Thus one could talk about the townspeople as representing ego caught in a self-deception and directing a false individuation process. The illusion of development is symbolized in the art, music, and developed political and ceremonial system, a new-age version of the German culture prior to World War II. The ego illusion is manifest in the split-off complex of the scapegoat child and the consequent separation of shadow from self system. Yet that part of the psyche represented by the ones who walk away is still in touch with the transcendent function. This link with the true self forces rejection of a developmental process in which disparate and painful elements of the psyche are projected rather than integrated.

As useful as a detailed amplification of this kind might be, it also bypasses the question posed by Le Guin, a question as political as it is personal, as related to groups as to individual development. There are true and false modes of growth within the body of a community, just as there are true and false modes of growth within the body of an individual, and the two processes are related.

The Omelas story depicts three modes of relationship between individual and group, which we might label the townspeople, the scapechild, and the walkaways.

The townspeople of Omelas are Le Guin's modern, spiritualized yuppie everyman and everywoman. They use the community to serve their individual needs—material, aesthetic, ecstatic, and spiritual. To do this, they begrudgingly accept the suffering of the scapechild because they know it is necessary for the continuance of their lifestyle. Yet no matter how creative and artistic they feel, there is always something missing. We might say that they have strayed from the path of individuation because a part of themselves, their shadow, is always cut off from the self. Their shadows are projected and then identified with the scapechild, who holds their dark side for them and suffers for their sins. They are like Christians who derive spiritual sustenance from overt dependence on a scapegoat Christ, a Christ who sacrificed himself in order to redeem mankind's sins. Men and women in such a relationship to a messianic scapegoat, no matter how many good works they perform as individuals, are part of a group that creates and sustains suffering and irresponsibility. The townspeople's passive acceptance of the scapechild reinforces denial of their own and others' shadows. Despite the Omelas townspeople's cultural and social achievements, they are only slightly more developed than the Germans before World War II and other racist societies such as our own in America, to the extent that Omelas is conscious of how and why they are using the innocent child for their personal and collective gain rather than hiding behind a political or spiritual ideology, as we so often do, a dubious distinction but perhaps a developmental step.

The second mode of individual-group relationship is that of the innocent, unconscious scapechild itself. We know that conscious acceptance of the scapegoat role in the group may indeed be a part of the individuation path. Asserting one's own individuality at times requires defying the group and accepting its approbation, even its most extreme penalties. Christ and the other Hebrew prophets were men and women who took on the corrupters and the moneylenders and suffered the most extreme consequences. But in Le Guin's story, the scapechild is the pure innocent. It is a victim who is not to blame, one who cannot be psychologically relativized as "deserving" his or her fate, as has been done to so many scapegoats who stand in our stead, be they the "greedy" Jew, the "stupid" black, the "corrupt" Italian, the "undeveloped" cancer or "perverted" AIDS patient. Le Guin uses a child as the symbol of the pure victim. We use the severely mentally ill or the developmentally disabled, the drug-addicted infants and other "innocent" victims to siphon off our darkest, guiltiest thoughts, feelings, and actions.

14

Finally we come to the mode of individual-group relationship portrayed by the walkaways, that subgroup blessed or cursed with the burden of what James called an "independent sort of emotion" as well as the ability to act on that emotion (Le Guin 1975, p. 224). Le Guin gives them a romantic send-off in her story. But who are they in relation to the group? Are they really heroes? Are they themselves victims, brothers and sisters to the scapechild whose fate moves them so? Or can they become something more than either hero or victim?

It is certainly easiest to identify with the walkaways as spiritual heroes, individuals who fulfill the needs of the group for honesty and incorruptibility. Those who take that role may experience themselves as being on the path of self-development. A subgroup of these people could certainly be called heroic individualists, people with the courage not to live in a society which so blatantly compromises its own values and who leave the group and its collective limitations behind in their quest for self-knowledge, meaning, and wholeness, no matter what the risks. In the wilderness, the individual confronts the transpersonal, the unknown. It is the place where the shaman, the healer, and the prophet go to struggle and eventually gain wisdom and power.

Some of the walkaways of Omelas can certainly be such individuals, those who forsake the group to begin the individuation process. But so often the most developed of these conscious heroic walkaways themselves end up as victims of a profound scapegoating process. A revered teacher of mine at Harvard Medical School, Professor Q., now deceased, was a prominent neuropsychiatrist in Berlin when the Nazis threatened to close all the universities in which Jews were allowed to teach. As we now know, many students and professors, like the townspeople of Omelas, accepted this scapegoat situation not only as the price for continuing their work but also as a reward, for the Jews that left tenured and other prestigious positions allowed them to move rapidly up the academic hierarchy. Professor Q. was one of the few non-Jews who felt he had to walk away in order to live a life of integrity. Perhaps the fact that he had a harelip and had always felt a connection with the innocent victims of society gave him the courage to act. Or perhaps he identified too strongly with the scapegoat for his own good, for he was profoundly victimized for his stance. He lost tenure, professional standing, and finally all personal freedom when he was arrested. After many months in prison, he was released on the condition of emigration without money, property, or proof of medical training. It took him fifteen years to regain professional standing and license. Years later, he returned to lecture in Germany for a month. He told me how he was struck by the number of former colleagues in the psychological and medical fields who continued to benefit by not having walked away as he did. He was particularly cynical about the work of his psychoanalytic colleagues. Perhaps he was envious or perhaps he was sensing their unhealed wounds. Creature comforts, social esteem, and the cultural advantages of a well-organized society seemed to win out in most individuals even if they relied on something as horrible as concentration camps for balance. When faced with the realities of sacrifice, few of us turn out to be the heroic saints of our fantasies.

The individual who assumes the scapegoat role always feels victimized. Despite his or her personal valence for that role, despite a conscious or unconscious desire for individuation implicit in societal exclusion, the unbearable emotional onslaught engendered by excommunication from group life will inevitably overshadow personality and personal motivations. With few exceptions, the true scapegoat is forced along a path of fire to a fate that rivals the most heinous crimes against society. There are no prisons for scapegoats, there is no legal recourse, no hope for rehabilitation or reprieve. Rene Girard points out, in considering the unlikelihood of ever rehabilitating the scapegoat, that "if he turned out to be entirely innocent, then his persecutors would become the guilty ones. We would have a whole collection of vicious killers in his stead. And no one wants that" (1987, p. 97).

A certain kind of scapegoat, however, may return transformed into a messiah or savior, their sacrifice after all, having saved the community from its own conflict and potential destruction. The symbolic or real death and transfiguration of the scapegoat into messiah may end up saving the community from its collective guilt as well—that is its role and group mission—but it does little for individuals who suffer or even die to assuage the guilty sins of others. The scapegoat is not only a mythic figure but a very real flesh-and-blood victim of societal processes over which he or she has almost no control. In the last words of Jesus, "My

God, my God, why hast thou forsaken me?" we hear the sublime voice of the ultimate scapegoat-hero-messiah who suddenly faces his very human pain and mortality as he is simultaneously elevated to Godhood. Few scapegoats die heroes except in the eyes of future generations of worshipers. Those who remain alive in their scape-goathood also experience the acute sense of betrayal that Jesus' desperate words highlight so eloquently. Jesus is an archetype of individuating man; few humans can sustain such a fiery path.

The line between hero and victim can be very thin indeed. Let us consider those walkaways who are more victim than hero, those who unwittingly play out the scapegoat role, although not from within the scapechild's cage. These victims often feel like heroes. They are extremely sensitive to the evil and guilt of the society and feel deeply, personally burdened by injustice, so much so that they feel the imperative to leave even when they are not coerced to do so. But they are moved more by identification with the victim than spurred by the impetus toward fulfillment and individuation. They are the too sensitive teenagers, the run-aways from middle-class homes, the rebels without a cause, the battered and deprived who might cause trouble and therefore need to be excluded from the mainstream every bit as much as the scapechild needs to be excluded.

These walkaways carry our guilt but cannot bear the load. They are creations of the group more than self-creators. They may feel like heroes but they have too little self-development to take up the hero's way. They have unconsciously accepted the collective projection of the scapegoat without having the ego structures necessary to use the role for individual transformation. They do not do well in the wilderness. The wounds they sustain are too deep to heal. When they recover, if they recover, they do not return as heroes or messiahs, are not forgiven and reinstated into the community; they return to the place of victims, the slums and hospitals of our cities and towns.

Mario Savio, quintessential hero of the 1960s, led the Free Speech Movement at Berkeley and almost single-handedly brought that great university to its knees in the fight against the Vietnam War. He refused to accept the too acceptable hypocrisy of two levels of young citizens: those with no vested interests who were drafted and those with privilege who didn't have to go because they could get student deferrals or had fathers who found places for them in the National Guard. Savio was a brilliant philosophy graduate student with a student deferral, but he wouldn't be quiet, and that part of him was set up by the group of us who hated Vietnam but didn't go the whole nine yards to try to stop it as Savio did. The part of him that was scapegoat hero eventually destroyed the rest of him. His life since his brief ascendancy has been a long siege of mental hospitals, empty rooms, and street living. The group found him, pursued him, exalted him, exiled him, and eventually destroyed him. This is the distinction between those who *take on* the group's scapegoat as a first step toward integrating their own shadow and selfhood and those who *take in* the group's scapegoat and are ruled and destroyed by it.

There is yet another way in which the walkaway may be constellated: not as hero or victim but as interpreter or teacher, the conscious scapegoat. This third version is, in a sense, outside of Le Guin's image, for her walkaways do not return, while the interpreter or teacher must never really leave. These are individuals who neither accept a comfortable place in the scapegoat system nor put themselves beyond the human need that creates it. What distinguishes this response is that however much such individuals abhor the psychology of victimization, they are always fully cognizant of their own role in creating and accepting the scapegoat process that they abhor. Such knowledge makes it far more difficult to "walk away" as either a hero or a victim, although some may try to do so. More often they deal with their discomfort and guilt by seeking to understand and eventually communicate their own role in the collective. Like Le Guin herself, they find a way to do so in the role of artist, consultant, healer, or analyst. They locate themselves on the boundary of society, one foot in the wilderness and the other in the town square. Their interpretive stance—sometimes behavioral, at other times verbal—is a comment and an attitude rather than a prescription.

What I have called the interpreter or teacher takes much from the archetype of the Wise Elder. It is the Wise Elder in each of us that makes it possible to honor the dual reality of individual and group member. This may be the lesson from the apocryphal story of Buddha, who at the end of his seven-year quest attained enlightenment under the bodhi tree. At that moment he had the option of becoming one with the universe or returning to his human status to serve and teach. His choice was to serve, and this is a model of an individuated person, someone who serves himself or herself and the group from a place of self-knowledge. Without knowledge and acceptance of the group as part and parcel of one's identity, there is no service, and no individuation. We recognize this combination in someone like Mother Teresa and in all those less-publicized people who stay true to themselves and to their group, one in balance with the other.

How can we work to achieve this balance? A first step is to accept the task and responsibility of working towards an understanding of the group unconscious *in vivo*, not just as a metaphor for the unconscious collective in the individual. The human group is after all flesh and blood, a natural human phenomenon with both creative and destructive potential. It seems to me that only through detailed experiential knowledge of the collective unconscious of the group, such as we have worked toward in the individual and within the therapeutic dyad, can we guard against its destructiveness and learn to establish more appropriate conditions for a nurturing relationship between group and individual.

Jungian thought has a great deal to contribute to our pursuit of group knowledge if we can let go of our history of aversion to groups and attend to group and collective life with the same explorative zeal that we have for analysis.[3] But the most important question to explore concerns the relationship between individuation and service, for service in whatever form is always to and with the group, our human community. In one form of Tibetan Buddhist meditation, practice begins by contemplating the suffering in the world and ends by dedicating what has happened during the meditation to its reduction. Therapists might consider the same practice, that is, our work with our patients could hold in mind the supraordinate task of bettering the lot of humankind rather than furthering individual development separate and apart from group life.

We must also learn how to be a part of developing groups, and one way to do this is to accept what I have called the interpreter role within them. We must return from our individuation quests with knowledge for the group and knowledge about its role in helping us. We must be willing to speak up about what we think is wrong in our groups much as the analyst must deal with transference and countertransference relationships. Taking on an interpretive function in the groups in which we are members can be much more difficult in group life than in the dyad. It takes a special kind of courage because the stakes are very high. Groups deal with power, money, and survival. Talking about what happens in groups, particularly pointing out the scapegoat, often risks loss of position, security, even life. But this remains part of the risk and reward of individuation. To ignore what we each can do to help others in our quest for individual development is to miss the very essence of that quest.

2

The Development of Group Consciousness

W HEN MEDIATED THROUGH INTENSE GROUP EXPERIENCE, THE SCAPE-goat archetype is one of the most powerful determinants of human behavior. Life itself may be willingly sacrificed when we are in its grip. But the influence of group consciousness and the powerful group archetype that it calls into play are not only functions of extreme situations such as war, riots, and religious ceremonies. Humans are both individually conscious and a profoundly sentient species; most of our lives are lived in groups; much of our thoughts and feelings are evoked and colored by groups. Even as we are concerned for the development of our individual consciousness, itself a Western collective ethos, the influence and importance to group life and group consciousness extend to every nook and cranny of human circumstance.

In the service of emphasizing our individual identity, we have learned to separate individual consciousness states, often thought of as our "ordinary" reality, from non-individual consciousness states, including group consciousness. The latter tend to be consigned to either the "higher" realms of the spirit or the "lower" realms of the group and mass man, Jung's *abaissement du niveau mental* (1950, par. 226). Dividing human consciousness into such polar categories has a long psychological history dating

21

back to a time when the faculty of individual consciousness was interpreted as a divine gift separating humans from their animal nature. Such conceptualizations define us too rigidly by this gift; inflating the centrality of individual consciousness seems increasingly inapplicable to our postmodern world, which also requires and values that part of our nature that functions sentiently and creatively as a member of human groups and, more broadly, as a species member of our planet. How much richer to view our species as possessing the capacity for a variety of consciousness states ranging from individual consciousness to ecstatic merger states of group consciousness—a continuum of lenses through which we experience, understand, and enjoy our inner and outer world—a continuum which is itself a unique and evolving potential with our species.

Recent work in child psychology, particularly on the development of consciousness in infants and very young children, may be useful in appreciating the importance of this continuum in our lives. For hidden in their nonverbal behaviors are clues to a variety of consciousness states in which knowledge of individuality is unknown or unconscious. As far as we can tell, infants and very young children do not begin their lives with a developed ego or sense of "I-ness" but rather dwell in consciousness states that are far more fluid and merged. Since psychology is carried within a cultural bias which emphasizes individuality, it is not surprising that developmental psychology, too, has tended to focus on the exploration of how individual consciousness emerges from the more merged consciousness states of early life without a comparable interest in whether and how these early "non-I" states develop into part of our consciousness as adults. But given the general subject of this book, it seems important to use the considerable body of data on the early development of consciousness to speculate also on the possible childhood origins of merger states in adults.

The word *ecstasy* is formed from the Greek *ex*, meaning "out," and *histanai*, meaning "to cause to stand." *Ecstasy* literally means standing outside of one's person. Ecstatic consciousness can be looked at as a state in which one's personal boundary, one's "I," is diminished or lost through merger with something or someone else (Colman and Colman 1975, p. 7). If ecstasy can be thought of as a merger experience in which the personal identity is diminished or lost, then, in many ways, the dynamics of ecstasy reflect and invert the developmental dynamics of infant and child consciousness. Children struggle to develop out of a merged consciousness state by creating boundaries which emphasize their individuality, the very boundaries which the mystic and the ecstatic seek to suspend. Tracing the dynamics of this struggle could suggest a framework for studying a reverse process in adults, the process that leads to states of ecstatic merger, including group consciousness.

Most adults locate consciousness "inside" their individual identity. The notion of a consciousness that resides outside the individual ego is unfamiliar and counter to common sense, yet recently both ecological and psychological theorists have emphasized a more expanded definition. Group consciousness is a core concept of Bion's theory of group behavior. He found that "a certain cohesion is given to these anomalous mental activities if it is assumed that emotionally the group acts as if it had certain basic assumptions about its aims" (1959, p. 172). The basic assumptions (the formulations of which he labeled dependency, pairing, and fight-flight) are unconsciously shared by the group in a shifting pattern contingent on a variety of factors, including the difficulty of the overt task, the quality of leadership and followership, and the psychological valences of the members. These shared assumptions are seen by Bion as regressive operations used by the individual to defend against psychotic anxieties brought on by the fragmenting, boundary-dissolving effects of the group process. In this contact with the complexities of group life, the adult resorts to regressive mechanisms described by Melanie Klein (1959) as being typical of the earliest phases of mental life. Klein's formulations of the primitive defenses in infancy, including mechanisms such as splitting and projective identification, are for Bion the regressive states that are defended against by individuals through the basic assumptions, thereby creating the common group mentality.

Other group theorists have elaborated the idea of a shared group consciousness. Bion's notion that the group can be unconsciously perceived by its members as a maternal entity has been referred to by others in terms of a preoedipal mother: "the perception of the group as an ever waiting, potentially symbiotic mother" (Gibbard, Hartman, and Mann 1974, p. 90). From a slightly different perspective, the group may be perceived as a transitional object of the kind Winnicott (1953) describes, with its psychological mechanisms linked to that stage of child development. Jung's concepts of the collective unconscious and the transcendent function are particularly helpful in understanding certain ego states and merger experiences that transcend the individual psyche.

The concept of merger is a literal metaphor for one's origin; we start life as dependent beings fused with the physiology of another person. There is no "I" at the beginning. We do not answer to our own name, the symbol of our separateness, until much later. The process of emerging from the womb into the arms and then the lap, the playpen, the yard, of going from the yard to the school and finally leaving home is one of continuously increasing individuation. A central theme of human development from conception to the height of adolescence is becoming an individual, feeling unique, experiencing a recognizable and more or less constant identity.

But as important as the struggle for individuality is—and although such consciousness has, in general, served our species adaptation—it is not necessary to assume that individuality is the only desirable goal in development. In striving for uniqueness and separateness, we may submerge or even ignore important parallel developments in consciousness which are continuous with our more diffuse origins—our earliest states of consciousness.

In *Civilization and Its Discontents*, Freud described "early phases of ego-feeling" as the precedent of oceanic feelings described by many people. He suggested that "the origins of the religious attitude can be traced back in clear outlines as far as the feeling of infantile helplessness" (1930, p. 72). Jung, too, had a similar equation in mind when he wrote about the "thoughtless state of early childhood, where as yet no opposition disturbed the peaceful flow of dawning life, to which the inner longing always draws us back again and again" (1943, par. 65). Many philosophers and psychologists have recognized that this early merged consciousness of infancy may hold the key to an entire range of ecstatic and mystical experiences and phenomena, those sought after and those that invade everyday reality. Many mystical and ecstatic traditions allude to fetal and infantile consciousness as the prototypes of spiritual bliss. It is not by chance that our most

24

common metaphor for describing mystical experience and its effects on the personality is "rebirth" or "born again." When we try to imagine what it was like to be an infant, we rely on our memories of ecstatic states, for we cannot be sure we are remembering our own infancy. However, for all their similarities, ecstatic experience is not merely the recapitulation of infantile experience, anymore than love is the recapitulation of the oedipal complex. To say so would be to deny the importance of experience beyond the toddler state in shaping that experience. In these ecstatic states, we are likely to experience a sense of merger or union with something outside our personal boundaries: God, the cosmos, nirvana. This is the reunifying experience of the adult. Rebirth in mystical experience is both metaphor and reality, an attempt to regain a sense of wholeness, of merger, of being cared for, that was one's earliest condition.

In the past thirty years, child psychologists interested in studying the development of consciousness have attempted to integrate psychoanalytic theory based on adult speculations about very early states of consciousness, as exemplified by the earlier quotation of Freud from *Civilization and Its Discontents*, with field observations of actual infant and child behavior. In general their findings suggest that adequate infant-mother bonding and stage-appropriate interaction in a coherent and emotionally responsive social environment are the necessary building blocks of consciousness. Recently, more detailed infant research has begun to elucidate models of early development which postulate the step-by-step acquisition of consciousness within a field of human interaction. Again, most of this work is focused on the acquisition of individual consciousness, but there is much to be learned and interpreted from this work regarding non-individual consciousness as well.

There are two major theoretical perspectives which order the emerging models of infant development and bear directly on the development of ecstatic states in infancy. One, best exemplified by the work of Michael Fordham, holds that the psychological infant, in utero and at birth, is "significantly separate from its parent, and needs, if it is to survive, to make a relation with her by taking an active part in bonding with her" (1993, p. 7). The second, best exemplified by Margaret Mahler (1972), holds that there is a minimal psychological differentiation between mother and infant at birth; separating out from this symbiotic merger is the critical task for the development of consciousness. Both perspectives are useful for our purposes since they postulate that the development of individual consciousness requires a psychological process that takes place in a variety of "non-I" states. I have found Mahler's approach to be heuristically valuable to our inquiry because it emphasizes the dominance of symbiotic merger states in the early child experience compared to Fordham's emphasis on individual identity. It also is closer to my own observations of the psychic development of children. However, before considering her approach, let me summarize some of Fordham's valuable insights as they apply to the development of group consciousness in children and adults.

Fordham postulates infant separateness and psychological wholeness from the very beginning of his or her life in utero. As Naifeh puts it in his excellent review of Fordham's theory, "the fetus is essentially a separate, individual self who comes fully formed into relation to the mother and the external world" (1993, p. 13). Fordham sees the breakdown of this initial wholeness, the infant self, as critical to survival. He calls this process "deintegration," an adaptational process which occurs whenever the organism comes into relation to the environment beginning with the earliest moments of the fetus activity in utero. The self mediates this deintegration process; the "deintegrates" that are formed draw on the archetypal patterns that are a preprogrammed part of the infant makeup and "reintegration" occurs as part of a new, more adaptable state of being which now features more complexity and less homogeneity. This process of deintegration/reintegration is, for Fordham, equivalent to the individuation process itself, one that begins in utero and continues throughout child and adult life.

Although most of Fordham's reflections on the development of consciousness are framed through an emphasis on the infant's individualness, his scheme does consider other states of consciousness, particularly the child's relationship with the collective unconscious. Thus deintegration always includes developing connections with aspects of the infant's environment and his or her archetypal nature. "Inasmuch as an infant self uses archetypal deintegrates in his adaptation to his mothering environment and develops the dichotomy of conscious-unconscious, his ego may be said to come into relation with the collective unconsciousness expressed in pre-personal part objects" (Fordham 1985, p. 49). In this process, the individuating child "specializes parts of himself" according to what is needed by the individual (ibid., p. 91). The self, acting through its deintegrates, takes in what is needed and available from the culture and the collective, at first whole, undigested, and largely unconscious, and later, under the aegis of individuation, more assimilated, and integrates it into the personality. We might postulate, using Fordham's theory, that the ongoing relationship between the developing child and the external group structures he or she encounters is mediated through the group archetype, in the form of a deintegrate. For example, the child encountering the family group in a way that challenges his or her current psychic structure could take in "groupness" much as the child takes in "motherness." The group archetype orders the new data until assimilated sufficiently to reintegrate into the mosaics of self and emerging ego. Fordham himself does not deal with the development of group consciousness or the relationship between the individual and his or her group identity. Moreover Fordham postulates only limited relationship with archetypal forms in early life: "most of the dynamic images of the collective unconscious are far more complex structures than anything an infant can know" and must await his becoming related to the wider society outside the family (ibid., p. 49).

For Fordham, infant consciousness is in a continuous flux between pre-personal identifications and more holistic self-representations, and it is out of this tension that individual identity strengthens. The baby is "capable of quite a spectrum of experience. He does not just function in a continuous state of primitive identity in which subject and object cannot be distinguished and where thought and action are one" (ibid., p. 54). One wishes that he would say more about when the infant does function this way! However, Fordham, ever the individualist, focuses on the early roots of uniqueness rather than those of merger and does not follow any of the other "spectrum of experiences" into adulthood. His theory, through the evolving dynamic of deintegration/reintegration, does describe the outlines of a process through which the collective unconsciousness and the social environment is incorporated through the individuation process into the emerging structures and spectrums of consciousness.

Mahler's work (1972) and the work of other developmental psychologists in her school differs significantly from Fordham's because of her postulation of mother-infant symbiosis as the earliest self experience and her interest in this and other merger states which precede individual identity and consciousness. In her sequence, the infant moves through four basic stages of the development of consciousness before emerging with a sense of "I" or ego consciousness. From an initial stage of minimal differentiation, it gradually discriminates between those parts of the world which are part of its basic internal reality and those which are outside its being and neutral to its existence. At each stage, it comes closer to experiencing the boundaries of its own being and interacting with others as distinct persons; learning to recognize "I" leads to learning to control relationships with "you."

Following Mahler's and my own work, I describe four epigenetic ecstatic merger states occurring in infancy, which predate individual consciousness and which form a developmental base for later consciousness states: group consciousness, individual consciousness, and the myriad of other consciousness states that make up the variety of human experience.

The first stage, the fetal experience, is a merger with totality psychologically undifferentiated from and physiologically fused with the mother; the fetus has no perception of personal boundaries or the limits of being. He or she is literally at one with the world, a totally connected, dependent organism, virtually a subsystem of the mother, yet growing to an inner tune of his or her own. The boundaries between mother and fetus are regulated by a feedback so exquisite that from the beginning, separateness must be defined in terms of dependence. Such is the physiological reality of the prebirth state. We can only guess at the psychological reflection of fetal existence, dominated as it is by an immature nervous system. Some psychological theorists believe that these experiences are "remembered" in nonverbal ways which later affect emotional patterns. In recent psycho-spiritual techniques such as active imagination, "rebirthing," and holotrophic breathing, fetal consciousness is deliberately sought as a gateway to here-and-now ecstatic experience. Whether we are dealing with remembrance or metaphor is difficult to discern, but the fetal position and fetal memory occur often enough in adult life that it is difficult to ignore the possibility of trace memories, of subjective ties to our earliest experience.

Once the infant begins to perceive the outside world, he has moved to the second stage of consciousness, merger in the dyad. Infant and mother are now a true "symbiotic" dyad. The infant begins to perceive boundaries of self, but these are vast and diffuse and definitely include the mother in the self part. We cannot be sure how and why this momentous change occurs. But it is most likely developmental: a maturing nervous system encountering the typical infant's environment and experience gradually makes more and more differentiations. Mahler suggests that the motive for making an initial discrimination between the dyad and the outside world lies in the infant's awareness of the good, warm, secure experience consistent with mother's presence and that of the bad, cold, insecure experience that occurs when mother is not present.

Once the baby shows a definite preference for her mother, she is signaling an awareness of the two distinct parts of the dyad; the experience of total merger is behind her and even the dyadic union is diluted. The infant is now likely to recognize friends, enemies, and neutrals, not only knowing more about what is happening inside the dyad but also beginning to react more to people outside the dyad. The infant begins to alternate between kinds of relating: she can relate to herself, to the outside world, or to her mother. When she can crawl, she can choose to leave her mother, to explore other objects and people. She can develop special relationships with additional members of the family, maybe seeking out a sibling or giving a special smile to father. The infant starts to incorporate other family members into the fleeting sense of self. They are no longer part of the negative not-us.

Thus within six or seven months, the infant enters a third stage of consciousness: merger in the group, the root of group and collective consciousness in adulthood. His boundary is being stretched to include significant others outside of the mother-infant dyad. Faces and gestures of individuals are observed and touched as if to find out who qualifies for entrance into this first and most sacred club of self. New persons in the infant's life are checked against the face and gestures of the mother, sometimes in wonderment and other times in despair. As the criteria for election to this "club" expand to include familiar faces and gestures belonging to others besides those of the dyad, the concept of outside also becomes more specific. The "stranger reaction," an apprehensive, anxious, startled response in the child when confronted with an unfamiliar face, develops sometime after six months and before one year. It signals an entirely new complex level of perception: the symbiotic dyad has been replaced by an inside, bounded self containing a mosaic of familiar persons, while the outside non-self contains individuals and objects recognized as not belonging.

It is difficult to imagine the subjective experience that corresponds to these developmental changes. The infant is no longer totally filled up with the merged world of mother-infant. Other people have become part of that consciousness. The child's new sense of inside is probably closer to a blend of gestures and faces, some of which are more linked to his or her sense of self than others. The primacy of the mother-child union in the child's world of self slowly gives way to a union with multiple others within the family environment. Where dyadic consciousness crystallized out of an earlier state of merger with totality, it now gives way to group consciousness.

The kind of primitive group self-consciousness at this stage of development might be analogous to the adult's experience of ecstatic involvement in a group ceremony. Adults can become so immersed in a group entity that their "I-ness" is virtually lost. Their behavior is then dictated by their role in the group and their thinking is experienced as part of a group mind. Individuals caught up in such experiences—examples of which include mobs, intense work groups, religious groups, athletic teams, and the like—perceive the nongroup outside as separate and apart. Individual identity is submerged in the group's independent life; the "I" becomes a fleeting, insignificant sensation. Participation in a group is an engrossing experience; the individual is literally lost in union with others.

The relative loss of "I" that is part of profound adult group experiences is tempered by an awareness of pressure by the group to conform and the loss of the self's ability to respond beyond the limits of the role dictated by the group. One may then experience a conflict between whether to "go with the crowd" and allow further submergence of the "I" into the group consciousness, or whether to emerge from the mass self as an individual. The obscurity of a group may provide a comfortable lack of responsibility. That same obscurity may also be a potent stimulus to search for an identity that will establish one's self above and beyond the group. This is the force which creates charismatic leaders, dictators, and even group consultants out of individuals who are particularly adept at accepting a prolonged loss of self. Their "I" readily becomes the group; they need the group to feel whole.

The child six to nine months old cannot yet experience this conflict between merging with the group and maintaining the "I" because there is not yet a true individual identity. He is just beginning to develop an ego boundary that encompasses more than the symbiotic dyad. This stage of primitive group consciousness, in which the self is experienced as a mosaic of the selves around him, furthers the separation from the original pair and heightens the embryonic individual identity. Only gradually, as the child experiences part of his own potential in each new piece of his mosaic self, does he begin to discover an "I" that is constant in all these situations.

For the child, this enlargement of self beyond the dyad increases the scope of her actions and makes her dependent on many other social configurations in addition to the maternal relationship. Like any other role player, she explores the potentials of each new group situation. The infant may begin to play with other children, showing independence with them in ways that would be impossible alone with mother. A unique set of behavior develops when the infant is alone with father or other parenting figures, who were rather distant in earlier infancy but who now become increasingly important. The infant may behave one way when alone with father and another way when mother is still in the room. She may "merge" in the family relationship by becoming "one of the kids" but find other times and ways to be acknowledged as herself, seeking her special place in the family society.

Out of the matrix of shifting group consciousness, a perception of uniqueness and separateness gradually crystallizes within the child: he develops a consciousness of "I." Every action and perception is newly individualized, seen for the first time with an individual pair of eyes. In such a state of consciousness, there is a precarious balance between awe and fear. The ego is increasingly devoted to the boundary with the external world, what can be done, how much achieved. The more diffuse, merged state of consciousness is relegated to a shadow world, a faint memory, that reemerges only in moments of regression. Yet the euphoric magic of the new state relies heavily on the subjective reality of merger to cover the fragile beginning of individuality—the naked, small, and helpless individual who must now encounter the frightening and unyielding world of people and things.

This individualization process takes place parallel to a similar crystallization of individual identity from the weakening dyadic symbiosis. It is likely that, for most infants, the dyadic merger is a more intense and resistant bond than the group merger, much as the adult's experience of group connection is often felt to be plastic and superficial compared to dyadic relationships such as love. This distinction between the dynamics of dyadic and group merger adds an important factor to the developmental process out of which individual identity is forged. It contributes to the continuum of consciousness between the dominating mother-child linkage of earliest life and the looser childhood connections of family and social groupings through to the final precipitation of a unique person capable of recognizing his or her separate existence and differences, apart from both mother and the various family constellations that supported his or her development.

In this sequence the developmental process by which the "I" emerges is more diffused and gradual than in Fordham's schema. It is also less specific about the psychic changes of early individuation as it applies to individual consciousness. But as I point out throughout this book, individuation in its fullest sense must finally include group consciousness or risk being synonymous with narcissistic individualism. For the developing child and certainly for his or her parents, the merger states described above may be relegated to a shadow world as delight in the newly emerging individuality (and its enormous adaptive rewards) takes over consciousness. But even if these merger states lose the ascendancy they had in infancy and earliest childhood, they continue on in the child's subjectivity; one only needs to be close to a child to appreciate how frequent they experience a variety of ecstatic states and how important they are in adaptation above and beyond their ongoing role in the development of individual consciousness (Colman and Colman 1975, pp. 93–126).

In other words, the variety of ecstatic states in adulthood do not develop *de novo*. They are part of a long developmental sequence in parallel and in concert with individual consciousness. Because our culture assumes the ongoing presence and hegemony of individual consciousness, when other states emerge as the dominant, it is usually with unexpected power and impact. We may mark these times as discontinuous but only if we have to believe that consciousness states other than individual consciousness are "extraordinary," not a part of our "ordinary" reality. But indeed what would "ordinary" life be like and how could we develop in breadth and depth without the impact of love, spiritual experience, and group life? all ecstasies which decrease the primacy of the ego and transcend the "I."

If psychologists have been little interested in pursuing these merger states in childhood, the same cannot be said of novelists and film makers, as William Golding's *Lord of the Flies* (1958) and Yukio Mishima's *The Sailor Who Fell from Grace with the Sea* (1965) attest. These and other works featuring frightening atavistic ceremonies spawned by group process in children are important and recurrent themes in art because we are still shocked by the intense sense of group identity that (re)emerges in latency with a power that rivals family and individual identity combined. We know little of how the group archetype, played out in the specifics of early group consciousness, emerges as a group complex in childhood and adolescence and effects group functioning in later years. It is possible, for example, that if this early phase of development is well managed through appropriate family and collective "integrates" and the group complex is in balance with other personality structures, the adult will be able to better tolerate the loss of individual consciousness and fear of loss of individual control that weighs so heavily in group experience. These are not abstract theoretical speculations. Leadership skills depend on such abilities; our human collective depends on both groups and individuals who function comfortably and creatively in both collective and individual realms. Moreover, the quality of consciousness which is found in our best leaders, their ability to function in many different states of consciousness, particularly individual and group consciousness, is also found in creative

33

people in general, whatever their field, however manifested, for creativity requires access to consciousness states that transcend the narrow focus of individuality.

In this developmental view, consciousness, like natural light, is multicolored even when it looks to be monochromatic. It is wave and particle even when it can be objectively measured as either. Much as a given light filter brings a particular color, vibrational energy, or particle size to the foreground, so too can a person experience the world from a panoply of subjective vantage points. In this view consciousness is like a slowly changing mosaic; how the different elements and substates combine, dissolve, and combine again is part of the mystery of development—a unique crystallization of the forces of nature and nurture. Thus the childhood of the Dalai Lama or Krishnamurti was a societally conceived training group for experiencing and appreciating the varieties of consciousness states available in such activities as trance, meditation, chant, song, and study—an educational environment quite different from that of most children of the West. But even more basic may be the infant's silent subjective experience, of which we can know so little. For no matter how we observe, theorize, abreact, or otherwise psychically explore early infant consciousness, it will at best remain as adult metaphor, and yet what happens in these months without words is the template that organizes the mosaic.

The infant's experiences as he moves through each merger state could subtly influence his tendency to seek out a particular kind of consciousness state of ecstatic experience in later years. Thus, an extended dyadic merger state in infancy might provide a desirable model for future love experiences, or it might be experienced by the young child as smothering and drive the adult to seek solitary or group modes rather than dyads. The lack of supportive mothering and family life may prod a child to look for ecstatic experience in solitary ways, or it might induce an enormous longing for merger with one other or with a group. Adults develop patterns for evoking ecstatic experience, for returning to that earlier world of union and merger, based in part on early positive and negative fixations or nodal points in the various prerelational states.

This does not imply that all adult ecstatic experience is childhood merger revisited, but only that the forms of adult ecstasies are powerfully influenced by the dynamics of these earlier states. No exact blueprint is possible here, only the likelihood that three years of prerelational consciousness provide the crucial framework for ecstatic life and ecstatic orientation in the future.

Evidence for this perspective is the frequency with which a given adult's psychological focus toward the more common ecstatic states, such as love, sexual merger, communal ceremonies, and a variety of other altered states of consciousness, may be quite consistent. For example, some adults are oriented toward totality. For them, ecstatic sex is cosmic sex, a Bach cantata, the music of the spheres: the object is universal myth rather than personal fantasy or physical sensation. Drugs induce ecstasies that feature fusion with nature or the universal deity, and religious experiences tend toward involvement with an all-encompassing religious system. Love is idolatry and idealization, the partner expanded to godhood. These adults strive for an experience patterned on their earliest infantile state of merger with totality.

Other adults are oriented toward the dyad. Ecstasy is shared and enhances the focus on capturing and expanding the experience of dyadic merger or, in other words, love. They search for a world consisting of a single other, and they desire to live with a sense of being united with a caring partner who shares their most intimate rhythms and makes their sense of self an expanded, dyadic awareness.

Yet other adults are oriented toward the group. For them, ecstatic sex is group sex, either in actuality or, more frequently, through fantasy or vicariously experienced and sublimated modern rituals. Music, meditation, or drug experiences are preferred in a group context; the commune, ceremony, or festival provides the ultimate setting to "turn on." Their religious experiences take place in churches rather than alone in nature. Their love affairs are with social causes and nationalistic movements. They strive toward an ecstatic state in which they are part of a network of selves functioning as a single merged entity.

Other individuals prefer the experience of a heightened "I," a feeling of intensified personhood. Sex is solitary, whether the partner is present or not. Religious experience emphasizes themes of personal power, responsibility, and awareness. Love is of one's body, one's person, one's individual development. The elation of heightened awareness is exhilarating, but the ecstatic state of true merger and loss of "I" in group, dyad, or totality may be perceived as negative or frightening.

The induction of ecstatic states almost always begins with the development of a heightened "I" in which, like the toddler, we are caught up in a powerful awareness of our body, our movements, our accomplishments, and our attachments to the world. To progress further into ecstatic consciousness, we divest ourselves of individuality, lose our awareness of boundaries and objects, and experience merger with our social and physical environment.

Group and dyadic merger states sometimes become vehicles of a sense of merger with totality. The individual first experiences union with the group or the other and then moves into an experience of merger with totality. This progression is represented visually in elaborate mandalas which may depict scenes of the pantheon in its outer boundaries, gradually crystallizing inward in ecstatic pairs, dancing or loving, until, more centered still, one finds a less figured, more abstracted image of harmony, often portrayed through a symbol of wholeness such as the Tao, the cross, or a circle. Similarly, ecstatic group ceremonies may move from communal praying, dancing, or singing through the elevation of a sacred pair in some sort of initiation, such as marriage, to a merging of all participants that leads to an intense sense of the whole.

For most of us, the boundaries between these ecstatic orientations are not rigid. We may enjoy various kinds of settings, whether in isolation, in pairs, or in a group. But we may also consistently seek out one or the other for our peak experiences. Solitary walks on the beach at sunset may be more enriching than romance or partying; prayer, singing, or sex may be better when shared with a single other rather than in isolation or with many others. One gravitates to a particular form of ecstatic experience because it feels better suited to who one is, and this is because it is also who one once was.

This chapter attempts to link who we are to who we were through the filter of group consciousness. It suggests a definition of human identity that is both individual and group and postulates a developmental goal within the species of awakening group as well as individual consciousness. Groups are specific entities in our lives, and group consciousness relates to group development in the same way as individual consciousness relates to individual development or dyadic consciousness relates to dyadic development; each is a particular filter for understanding a process. It is easiest to see how the stage of group consciousness provides the experimental framework for later group behaviors, such as those that evolve in school-age children and continue through adulthood. What is newly learned in latency are extrafamiliar group interactional skills, but the unconscious is already part of the child's developmental past.

But group consciousness also exists as an ecstatic state based on an archetypally based part of our psyche, the group archetype. Our relationship to this archetype is a critical thread in our development and will determine a great deal about each of our paths of individuation. Or from another perspective, the earliest encounter with collective life perhaps from inside the dyad, perhaps from an even earlier consciousness, precipitates a deintegration/reintegration process which draws the group archetype into the developing self just as the ego archetype is drawn into the developing self. This individual/group resonance haunts us throughout our lives. For how can we be an individual without being part of our human group, and how can we be part of humankind without being an individual?

There are several implications of this development theory of consciousness that I want to explore briefly. One is the potential for understanding the different dynamic importance of group and dyadic relationships for a given individual. Those persons raised in situations in which group and family life were early, powerful influences, in which the group archetype was intensely activated, may have very different attractions to group life as adults than those persons for whom the mother-child orbit was predominant. Obviously there can be no simple, one-to-one causality here. A child for whom mother was the critical link between merger and individuality may grow to adulthood frightened by the intensity of two-person relationships and find freedom in a lifestyle emphasizing multiple group situations. Similarly, a child raised in a large family with a primary linkage to group experience as a prelude to individuality may later yearn for the uninterrupted bliss of closeness with one other. Regardless, increased understanding of the relationship between dyadic and group merger states in early childhood should provide a firmer basis for making the developmental links between child and adult experience. And beyond the elucidation of individual development is the relationship of these ideas to cultural differences, for example, the relative importance given in a community or nation to group and extended family ties compared to one-on-one ties in early childhood. These variations in the developmental sequence suggest a framework for examining cultures along a continuum of "we-ness" and "I-ness."

Another implication involves the experiential modes used by adults to enter the "other world," whether for shamanic healing or group depth consultation. For example, the gradual induction of a state of group consciousness, which is required in order to enter and learn from the depths of a specific group, is in part a return to a familiar state of being, an earlier state in which consciousness was superimposed with group and the group was consciousness. The shaman and his modern counterparts who are comfortable with this "other world" must struggle not to lose individual consciousness in their journeys entirely but to maintain a bit of ego-consciousness in order to report back in their role as healer and interpreter, just as the infant must struggle to find that sense of individualness from out of group consciousness as part of normal development.

We can also relate the theory presented here to learning experiences that emphasize group process, with important results. For example, group experiences provide powerful personal growth experiences as part of the task of learning about group process and authority relationships. The form of these personal experiences is remarkably similar; the individual, after gradually becoming immersed in the group and feeling powerfully wedded to the group corpus, suddenly breaks free from this group consciousness with an accompanying acute, exhilarating sense of his or her own uniqueness and originality. Such experiences often have mystical or spiritual overtones; the individual is discovering and creating himself for the first time. These remarkable rebirths are adult experiences in their own right and can lead to major changes in personal values and goals. Yet they are also recapitulations of the initial experiences of individualization out of the group matrix, the first magical creation of what has been called the "ideal state of self" (Joffe and Sandler 1965, p.

394). Such personal experiences, spawned by the group process, may be treated as important but outside the group task, as in groups with a well-defined external task; or as a product to be manipulated, as in some evangelistic religious movements; or as an opportunity to support attitude change and growth, as in the treatment situation. However these experiences are used, it is of value to explore their origins and their importance in the developmental process.

Ecstatic experience is by its nature change producing, both to the individual and society. Its passionately conceived wider perspective shatters the individual's narrow focus and society's adaptive norms. As long as the designated and authorized ecstatics, such as artists, spiritual leaders, or religious institutions, hold these experiences for the rest of us, society is "safe." But when their boundaries bleed into the larger collective, and when there is also a large subculture which supports ecstatic experience, such as happened in the 1960s, there is a new potential for change—often discontinuous, disruptive change. This is particularly true when the group archetype is activated and group consciousness is enhanced, for political structures and societal norms are the congealed matrix of the group archetype, and group consciousness has the potential of reliquifying this matrix, preparing it for new concepts and forms. The progression from individual vision to group vision, from Buddha's enlightenment to a collective embracing of his ideas, from Chief Seattle's or John Muir's vision to the development of an ecological movement, is a historical record of the dance between individual and group archetypes played out in more or less receptive cultures. From the perspective of the group, these creative individuals are ciphering the images and ideas of the collective. But these visions can only be actualized when there is a creative intersection of individual and group consciousness, when there is harmony between these two manifestations of the larger human consciousness. The shaman's vision is neither his nor his tribe's. It is mutual, reciprocal, interdependent. Such is the vision of all leaders and all groups if they truly represent us.

From the evolutionary viewpoint, the perspective of species survival, the group archetype and group consciousness must inevitably stabilize and underlie all the remarkable developments that individual consciousness has brought. Ontogeny recapitulates phylogeny. Human evolution is biosocial evolution, and group consciousness is imbedded in the developmental process of our childhood as well as our species. From this perspective, the awakening enhancement of a reflexive group consciousness and the maturation of our group nature and its complexes have become critical to our survival and therefore the obligatory direction of evolutionary development. How we manage our sentience, how we manage our group relations within and between species, how we manage our species relationship with our environment, has become humanity's central task. For it is not the Earth which we must save, it is Us.

3

The Mysterious Connection between the Individual and the Group

Mario Vargas Llosa, the renowned Peruvian novelist and politician, begins a recent essay on South American politics with a historical vignette which also serves to introduce my subject, the mystery of the group. Llosa's concern is with the conquest of Tawantinsuyu, the Inca Empire, by a handful of Spaniards. In 1532 Francisco Pizarro and fewer than two hundred followers were able to deal a mortal blow to an empire that ruled more than twelve million people. The Inca Empire was not a primitive society made up of barbarians, nor was Pizarro a brave hero, as we may have been taught in elementary school. On the contrary, the Inca culture was highly evolved, with social, spiritual, and military systems that spanned half a continent. They had managed to eradicate many social ills, including hunger, while Pizarro was the head of a band of mercenaries bent on financial gain and conquest.

Why was this ancient empire so easily conquered? The popular notions often taught to Western students emphasize the supposed superstition of the Indian savage: the presence of strange horses and iron weapons led the Indians to think that the

Spaniards were gods. Llosa believes that this version serves Western supremacy/noble-savage mythology more than historical accuracy. Recent records and journals from both sides suggest other variables, particularly group and political structures which transcend superstition and technology.

> At the precise moment the Inca emperor is captured, before the battle begins, his armies give up the fight as if manacled by a magic force. The slaughter is indescribable, but only from one of the two sides. The Spaniards discharged their harquebuses, thrust their pikes and swords, and charged their horses against a bewildered mass, which having witnessed the capture of their God and Master, seemed unable to defend itself or even to run away. In the space of a few minutes, the army, which defeated Prince Huascar, the emperor's half brother, in a battle for rule, and which dominated all the northern provinces of the empire, disintegrated like ice in warm water. (Llosa 1990, p. 49)

Llosa explains that the messianic group structure of the Tawantinsuyu was more harmful to its survival than all the conquistadores' horses and iron weapons.

> As soon as the Inca, the figure who was the vortex toward which all the wills converged searching for inspiration and vitality, the axis around which the entire society was organized and upon which depended the life and death of every person, from the richest to the poorest, was captured, no one knew how to act. And so they did the only thing they could do with heroism, we must admit, but without breaking the 1,001 taboos and precepts that regulated their existence. They let themselves be killed. (Ibid.)

The Inca Empire, a gigantic, efficient, spiritual beehive of an organization, seems to have deprived its subjects of much of their personal autonomy. Llosa elaborates:

> Those Indians who let themselves be knifed or blown up into pieces that somber afternoon in Cajamarca Square lacked the ability to make their own decisions either with the sanction of authority or indeed against it and were incapable of taking individual initiative, of acting with a certain degree of inde-

pendence according to the changing circumstance. . . . But
these semiliterate, implacable, and greedy swordsmen, who
even before having completely conquered the Inca Empire
were already savagely fighting among themselves or fighting
the pacifiers sent against them by the faraway monarch to
whom they had given a continent, represented a culture in
which, we will never know whether for the benefit or the dis-
grace of mankind, something new and exotic had germi-
nated in the history of mankind. (Ibid., pp. 49–50)

Beneath the surface of this vignette is the complexity of two
cultures in collision, two cultures with totally different views of
the social nature of man and individual consciousness, views
which are still warring in our own culture's development as well
as in our minds. As Llosa says, "Almost five centuries later, this
notion of individual sovereignty is still an unfinished business"
(ibid., p. 51), an enigmatic remark to which we will return.

According to Jung's most frequently quoted view of group
life, the Inca defeat describes yet another example of what he
called *abaissement du niveau mental,* a catchphrase which summa-
rizes the homogenizing consequences to the individual of giving
oneself over to the group mind (1950, par. 226). For Jung, less
interested in group and community development, the cutting
edge of psychology was elsewhere, and until very recently, the
study of the group and the community has been a nearly taboo
subject in Jungian psychology and among Jungian analysts. In fact,
those of us who have used Jungian concepts to study group issues
have faced considerable suspicion and attack.[4] Yet theory will, in
some sense, always serve need, and our needs for a healing psychology today are very different from those Jung faced when he
was developing his ideas. It was from the context of his experience
that Jung saw the hope of humankind resting on individual development while consigning group psychology to the *abaissement du
niveau mental,* which prevents individuals from flourishing, drag-
ging them down to the lowest common denominator of human
function.

I do not believe any thoughtful person today can continue
to believe that human and world survival is located within a frame
that sees individual improvement alone as the unit of change and
hope. Surely collective life contains aspects of *enhancement du*

niveau mental to balance the *abaissement?* Let us then explore this question by studying the connections between individual and collective parts of human experience and, in particular, by learning how to balance our deep exploration of the individual with a depth psychology of the individual in the group and also, about which we know least, a depth psychology of the group in the individual.

Two vignettes provide further material for a beginning in this direction.

As I was writing a first draft of this chapter, I received a call from a well-known scientist, a person known for his individual brilliance as a researcher. He asked for a consultation to cope with the imminent breakup of his research institute, a large and world-renowned group of scientists working together on related questions. The details of my consultation with this group are, of course, confidential, just as in individual analysis.[5] What is relevant to this paper about their crisis is that these brilliant individuals expended so little energy on their collective and its processes compared to their intense concern for their individual scientific development. They operated in the best traditions of our individualizing world, allocating all of their resources to learning how to be better scientists, better professional men and women, and none to learning how to be a better scientific community. Such was simply not a matter of concern to them, until they faced a threat to their survival. When I asked how they had survived past crises, they said there hadn't been any, but on further questioning they noted that all previous threats had been headed off by their gifted leader, Dr. Z., when he was at the helm. He held the place together, they said; he did it consciously and at the expense of his own personal research. However, very soon after he retired, the quality of all their work suffered. A new leader had been brought in—a hotshot researcher with little declared interest in the institute as a collective. This choice represented the group's continuing ethos—improving individual expertise and production as the best hope for renewal—and the current crisis questioned this policy.

Another example can be found among candidates at an analytic training institute who complain when institute politics enter into their analytic work. They feel that in such situations the sacred analytic vessel is broken and their work is compromised. Most commonly this comes into focus during the evaluation procedure, in their meetings with the reviewing committees. The candidates often feel that their individual work, their spiritual quest, their individuation process, is contaminated by the workings of the committees. Most experience these group processes as an artifact unrelated to their personal individuation process and their personal evaluation. The analyst members often (I would say more often than not) agree with their analysands in this view. They know, of course, the persons on the committees and may have heard rumors about dissension in their ranks. So they separate their analysands' developmental needs from the process of the "blighted" committee's evaluation process and help the analysands strategize about how to get through without committing themselves, without giving themselves away, without speaking their personal truth.

In both examples, the underlying conscious assumption, as in Jungian psychology, is the sacredness of the individual psyche and the profanity of the group psyche. A corollary of this assumption is the danger of the group to the development of the individual. Just as the scientists view their development as occurring only within themselves and not among their collective, so too do the candidates and their analysts view development as an individual affair. Analysis is designed to be just that—an individual affair—although it is actually a dyadic affair but certainly structured as a very private affair. And in the best analyses, it is a private affair, insulated from intrusions.

However, the candidates of the analytic institute want something more from the institute than training opportunities or a referral base, just as the scientists want more than equipment and an organizational base for grants from their research institute. For example, candidates give up some of that cherished privacy simply by seeking membership, for not only is their analyst involved in the politics of the institute but their analysis and even their present and future choice of analysts is inevitably included in the reviewing process. Some candidates would say that this shouldn't be, that they never bargained for such intrusions, that all they wanted was training. They could get training and a more bounded analysis by choosing not to join an institute, rather educating themselves by picking and choosing from the institute's offerings and the other excellent educational resources in the community. But they join the institute for something else: they join in order to become members of a community that they honor and from which they want honor in return. To put it most obviously, they join in order to belong, to be members of the group. Their decision to apply means that, at the unconscious level at least, they have reached the developmental stage in which membership in a group is very, very important to them. Or, put in a personal developmental perspective, they join because there is something they need to learn about joining.

Have you ever noticed that tales of individuation, fairy tales, good novels and journals, always take the hero and heroine (and the reader) further than they intended to go? There are always the initial trials in which the hero toils and fights against over-whelming odds. But when these are overcome by luck and skill and courage and magic, when it all seems to be over, there is always something more, often just when the journey is over, just before the homecoming, or even after it. This is often when the group reappears, when the hero has left the battlefield and must live out his or her life without the ego-aggrandizing develop-ments that go with the Hero and Puer archetypes. This is when the great learning so often occurs, in the coda which turns out not to be a coda at all but the symphony itself, or a whole new kind of music. What has been learned in the quest must be shared with the collective, for the Hero is both a developmental stage and an archetype. Heroes may develop into leaders, or they may become old soldiers with too many stories to tell. But if they remain on the battlefield too long, they may become Puers, like Peter Pan, a grown-up child forever caught in rebellious play. The hero must return and re-ground with his or her group or a new, more relevant or needful group, in order to provide meaningful service to the collective. Among many other outstanding exam-ples of this are the struggles of Gandhi in South Africa before his ultimate work in India.

In the most ordinary terms, just when we think we are home free—that we've matured, understood, become independent—the collective, which was there all the time, waiting for our return—the family, the academy, the institute, the job, the club, the homeland, the nation—makes its demand. Try as we may, that demand cannot be put aside. It returns again and again until it is faced, understood, and worked through (not around). Out of this work comes something more than can be dreamed, quite literally, for dreams are past, present, and future and, in their future aspect, a preparation and a blueprint, a foreshadowing of the reality of living which anchors the life of the individual in the life of the collective.

Taking our dreams into our life and living them means sharing the dreams in the collective's consciousness. This sharing of our hard-won individuation and the dreams on which it is based may be first experienced as dilution, even abasement. But sharing our separateness with others makes what we have learned more corporeal, more connected, and eventually more potent. With this re-grounding, finding a way toward "right action" becomes more complicated than before but also more meaningful. An example in this category of experience is the nuclear scientist, heir to the alchemist, who must add to his work with the retort not only the spectrophotometer and cyclotron but the treacherous ethical decisions implicit in working on such projects as nuclear bomb or human genome research. Such projects require decisions and actions that go beyond the technical and creative challenges of math and biochemistry. They require subtlety and wisdom in the field of ethics, which were long ago consigned to the gods of sophomoric concerns. In this category, too, are the psychotherapists who want more training but find that the real learning comes from embroilment in corruptions which challenge their idealizations about their training analysts and their community. As the famous return of the enlightened Buddha to serve teaches us so poignantly, individuation must be consummated not only under the bodhi tree but also especially in the crucible of the imperfect human collective.

Spiegelman writes about the sense of descent that accompanies this part of the individuation journey:

> Since I returned to membership in the Los Angeles Society a few years ago, I found that almost every new graduate goes through a final darkness and frustration with the administration or some authority and comes out with the feeling that he or she would do just as well, or even better, by not being a member at all. (1988, p. 142)

How much easier never to face any of this darkness and frustration which is so much a part of our collective life. One might as well not involve oneself in childbirth, parenthood, politics, love, or the sacred. The mysteries of individuation are not found only on the paths at the edge of the wilderness that end in the dark caves, abandoned huts, and hidden temples. The path of individuation is strewn with memories—one's own and those of others who have gone before, the elect who help and guide—which make one's own journey meaningful. Even more, the path is full of real people and difficult tasks, rife with complexity, littered with joyful as well as corrupt connections which embody the great, dark, deep essence of living. The initiations that mark the choice points of individuation begin not only in isolation but also in the group, and having tasted the group flesh, we cannot go back to defining ourselves by our individual nature alone, for that was never our only nature but the very illusion that initiation challenges, the illusion of the primacy of individual consciousness.

Consider this phrase, the illusion of the primacy of individual consciousness: it is a heresy to the Western way of life and to Western psychology, including Jung's contribution to it. Our depth psychology—Jungian, Freudian, and all their derivatives—has flourished in Western culture because we are a culture committed to the final flowering of the vision of the Age of Enlightenment, to supporting, even worshiping, the jewel of individual consciousness in each of us. In developmental psychology, many lifetimes of research have been devoted to chronicling the day-by-day, month-by-month, year-by-year path through which the small spark of individual knowledge and consciousness grows to independence, to individual reliance and centeredness. In analysis we expand and deepen this process of individuation by exploring the unconscious and the spiritual.

But we could just as well have tried to define the development of collective consciousness, the development of that part of us that begins in simple dyadic merger and moves through sibling consciousness to a wider and more complex consciousness of continuity, entanglement, and connectedness within our own species and beyond our species to other species and to our habitat. We could add to our study an exploration of the unconscious collective, the spiritual collective, and the ecological collective. We would then have a developmental and unconscious psychology of collective consciousness—intergroup, interhuman, interspecies consciousness—to balance the individual focus we have thus far taken.

Re-creating this balance should not be thought of simply as an intellectual exercise. I have suggested that it is part of the individuation process itself, particularly once the heroic journey diminishes and other archetypes come to the fore. For example, even as we functionally define individuation as a process of becoming fully and wholly oneself without compromise to society, there is a sense in which, as an individual grows in that direction, he or she also becomes more conscious and involved with the surrounding world. But this involvement is not the hero's involvement; there is a new relation to the collective captured in the archetype of the Wise Old Man or Wise Old Woman as advisor and guide, intervention based on knowledge of self rather than demand of the ego. We have many examples of this kind of intervention in Jung's writing, most notably in his descriptions of the archetype of the Wise Old Man:

> Often the old man in fairy tales asks questions like who? why? where? and whither? for the purpose of inducing self-reflection and mobilizing the moral forces and more often still he gives the necessary magical talisman, the unexpected and improbable power to succeed. . . . But the intervention of the old man—the spontaneous intervention of the archetype—would seem to be equally indispensable, since conscious will by itself is hardly ever capable of uniting the personality to the point where it acquires this extraordinary power to succeed. (1948, par. 404)

Perhaps the best human community "intervention" based on the knowledge of self is contained in Jung's story of the rainmaker, related by Barbara Hannah:

> Richard Wilhelm was in a remote Chinese village which was suffering from a most unusually prolonged drought. Everything had been done to put an end to it, and every kind of prayer and charm had been used, but all to no avail. So the elders of the village told Wilhelm that the only thing to do was to send for a rainmaker from a distance. This interested him enormously and he was careful to be present when

the rainmaker arrived. He came in a covered cart, a small, wizened old man. He got out of the cart, sniffed the air in distaste, then asked for a cottage on the outskirts of the village. He made the condition that no one should disturb him and that his food should be put down outside the door. Nothing was heard of him for three days, then everyone woke up to a downpour of rain. It even snowed, which was unknown at that time of the year.

Wilhelm was greatly impressed and sought out the rainmaker who had now come out of his seclusion. Wilhelm asked him in wonder: "So you can make rain?" The old man scoffed at the very idea and said *of course* he could not. "But there was the most persistent drought until you came," Wilhelm retorted, "and then—within three days—it rains?" "Oh," replied the old man, "that was something quite different. You see, I come from a region where everything is in order, it rains when it should and is fine when that is needed, and the people also are in order and in themselves. But that was not the case with the people here, they were all out of Tao and out of themselves. I was at once infected when I arrived, so I had to be quite alone until I was once more in Tao and then naturally it rained." (Hannah 1976, p. 128)

The spirit behind such interventions in community is captured in the *Tao Te Ching*, the great book of Taoist philosophy (Mitchell 1988). The genius of this little book is its absolute pragmatic commitment to the seamless flow between individual and collective, between spiritual development and organizational governance. Thus:

Know the white,
yet keep to the black:
be a pattern for the world.
If you are a pattern for the world,
the Tao will be strong inside you
and there will be nothing you can't do.
(p. 28)

And again:

Do you want to improve the world?
I don't think it can be done.

The world is sacred
It can't be improved.
If you tamper with it, you'll ruin it.
If you treat it like an object, you'll lose it.

The Master sees things as they are,
Without trying to control them.
She lets them go their own way,
And resides at the center of the circle.

(p. 29)

These quotes, like the whole book, are not about retreat from the world into oneself but about involvement based on knowledge and concern for self and collective. They talk to the power of men and women as leaders who have found their own personal and collective ways and are ready to help other persons and institutions find theirs. Beginning in 1987, I spent three years as president of the A. K. Rice Institute, a professional organization with a powerful and provocative membership. The *Tao Te Ching* was my constant companion; I don't know if I could have survived the job without it, although Machiavelli's *The Prince* came a close second.

In the same vein, at the end of his life Jung talked about the need to reforge the balance between individual and collective. In the very last paragraphs of *Memories, Dreams, Reflections*, he talks about his own rather startling shift, guided perhaps by the psychology of advanced age.

> The archetype of the old man who has seen enough is eternally true. At every level of intelligence, this type appears and its lineaments are always the same, whether it be an old peasant or a great philosopher like Lao-Tsu. This is old age and a limitation. Yet there is so much that fills me: plants, animals, clouds, day and night, and the eternal in man. The more uncertain I have felt about myself, the more there has grown up in me a feeling of kinships with all things. The fact it seems to me that if that alienation which so long separated me from the world has become transferred into my own inner world, and has revealed to me an unexpected, unfamiliarity with myself. (1965, p. 359)

This remarkable statement points to a view of wholeness and individuation that is very close to the ecological sense of wholeness

51

now emerging in modern philosophy as set forth, for example, by Thomas Berry in his book *The Dream of the Earth*. Berry is concerned with the same individualistic alienation from the world about which Jung writes. He sees it as part and parcel of humanity's "anthropocentric society"—our focus on the specialness that sets us apart from the rest of the planet. "In relation to the earth, we have been autistic for centuries" (Berry 1988, p. 215). Berry's viewpoint is based on a spirituality grounded in "the unique and irreplaceable qualities of the individual and the inseparable bonding with every other being in the universe" (ibid., p. 120). He suggests as part of the healing process that "we renew our human participation in the Grand Liturgy of the universe" (ibid., p. 215).

What Jung hints at in the above quote and what Berry and other ecological philosophers are setting forth for us in prophetic and apocryphal form is a view of wholeness larger than individual wholeness. It is a concept of wholeness based on a Self which includes the cosmos, solar system, Earth, and all the species that inhabit Earth without any notion of a hierarchical preference for humanity. In such a view, individual human consciousness is simply one characteristic of our species, like the flight of birds, the ability of fish to live underwater, bats' use of sound to measure distance, or bees' altruism in their reproduction cycle. Human consciousness has power, awesome power, and we must develop it as best we can, for it is part of our nature, but this does not give it overarching value in the web of connectedness that is our true context of experience and existence.

This newly emerging view of collectivity in the universe is close to the shamanic notion of reciprocity, which emphasizes our actual interdependent relationship to everything in and around us. Thus, what was only recently an anthropological oddity is now a powerful archetype in our body politic. All these developments point to the necessity of balancing what, in my view, is an inflated perception of the importance of individual consciousness in our species with exploration and development in the sphere of collective consciousness.

We know very little about this collective consciousness in ourselves or in others, and because we know so little, we appraise it with a child's eye. We want it to be there on a primitive, simple, comfortable level. We are happy when it helps, oblivious when it is silent, and angry when it deflates or punishes. Our undifferentiated and childish yearning for a suitable and simple collective reflects our yearning for a benign individuality. Why, we often ask, does our individual sense of ourselves not always feel like the joyous, ecstatic toddler? Why does it contain anxiety and doubt? Why does joy always seem to come out of suffering and pain out of pleasure? Why not stay an addict, sucking at the mother's breast, when it feels so bad to unglue the mouth and learn to speak, to try to get what is wanted and then meaningful?

It is no wonder we are so often disappointed and angry at the collectives we encounter—directly and knowingly—when they don't serve our needs, don't help us but cause us pain, when (as Spiegelman observed) we find something else, something we didn't expect and know little about. The scientist, the candidate, all of us who are curious, whose passion or profession is to explore, are horrified to discover that initiation and membership, which have always seemed interesting but secondary aspects to an individual career, are far more important than suspected. The new members of the institute, academy, or other seminal group find that their expectations were naive, and unless they are open to the mystery of and opportunity in what they actually find, they begin to wish for another group reality, or none at all.

Spiegelman reports his own experience.

> I can find some satisfactory mode of connection with almost any member of our group on an individual basis, but as a collective, this is most difficult and frustrating. What a paradox! All these individuation-pursuing and self-realization-promoting people have a difficult time being with each other except on an individual basis! It would seem we lack, on a group level, the kind of vessel that analysis itself provides, whereby consciousness, truthfulness, and relationship are deeply served. (1988, p. 143)

And he might have added that groups are not there only to serve individuals but to be served by them as well. And if groups were formed in the image of the analysis, what new would be learned from them?

Given our individualistic culture, the scientist and the candidate rarely consider that the cutting edge of their professional creativity and development might take place within the vessel of the group, as well as or instead of within the boundaries of their individually defined identity. And here I am not referring to learning *from a group*, taking something from it for oneself, but learning *as a group*, becoming something else as part of the encounter. In fact, we know little of how group encounters work in human development, only that they are profoundly important to most of us no matter how insulated, protected, or controlling an individual may be. We are often surprised and confused when encounters with the academy, the examining board, the IRS, the law, or the military change our lives. Usually only afterward, if ever, do we come to appreciate that these encounters were not adventitious experiences to be endured but part of our fate as sentient and collective beings.

Like all great mysteries, that part of the initiation process that occurs within the group cauldron is rarely polite or predictable.[6] When we fully encounter the collective—and here I speak particularly of confrontation with scapegoating and other sacrificial processes embedded in the initiation aspects of the group—we become inextricably and unmercifully enmeshed in group and organizational forces that are beyond us. It can be as ruthless and awesome as a full encounter with one's self and, like that encounter, it neither should be nor can be delayed or avoided; if this encounter is forestalled, we lose part of our selves and our potential for having turned our backs on our sentient nature and its mystery.

The fall of the Inca Empire is a most poignant illustration of the extreme vulnerability of a collective based on the scapegoat/messiah myth. Despite the complexity of this social and religious system and its focus on social justice, it was dependent on a godlike leader whose murder was ruinous to the whole culture. As Llosa, and the colonial history of South America, suggests, that kind of collectivity is no match in the short run for one based on individual sovereignty. Neither, however, is the verdict in on the ultimate worth of a system that, along with its predatory nature, elevates the individual and individual consciousness to a kind of religion which justifies cultural genocide.

In the two examples I have presented, we can also see some very negative practical consequences of an unbalanced focus on the individual. In the first example, the scientists had difficulty conceptualizing the importance of their collective process to their individual research. With one side of their psyches, they denied its importance. With the other side, like the Incas, they projected the care of a vital part of their reality, their collective reality, onto a wise and nurturant leader. In the scientists' nascent mythology, based on the ancient archetype of the scapegoat/ messiah, it was Dr. Z.'s great sacrifice (of his time, his own research, himself) that saved them and his loss that plunged them into the current crisis. In the second example, the candidates are half wise; they are more aware of their collective, more afraid of it, and also more judgmental toward it. They see the collective as intrusive and dangerous, something from which they must be protected. Their analysts tend to agree with the candidates, even though the evaluation process is their own creation and for the good of their community.

To fulfill our potential as humans is the unifying principle, the hope, the great motivator of our species. And in our full potential we are not separated I's. Each individual is also part of the group, and each group is a unity with its own mysteries and its own journey toward wholeness. This large conscious and unconscious collective and its embodiment in these mysterious groups is not simply a holding ground for individuals. The group, like the individual, is a vital organism in its own right, just as the adrenal gland is an organ with functions and processes beyond each endocrine cell. As for every life-encompassing system, the group has its own origin, its own process, its own stages of development, its own myths. Jung's premise about the reality of the psyche, the collective unconscious, can be paraphrased thus: we, this group that we are, is an awareness we all share, one that profoundly affects us at the most fundamental levels (1958, par. 655).

The power of our collective reality is well documented by many experiments and observations from the social sciences, which describe how perception and judgments differ from within different groups and how group membership and the attendant group consciousness affect individual performance. These effects are usually judged to be negative, for example, in Janis's work on political systems (1950), about which he coined the phrase "group think," and Deikman's work on cults (1990). Often forgotten is how group and individual effects are paired in almost all creative endeavors. The separation we make between the two is an artifact of our concentration on the individual.

Almost every individual effort of worth and substance is also a collective effort, be it a symphony orchestra, a think tank, an athletic team, a research group, a political assembly, or a supportive family. Shakespeare's theater company, Napoleon's armies, and basketball superstar Michael Jordan's teammates are not adjuncts but essential. Individuals require creative collectives for their fulfillment just as collectives require creative individuals for theirs.

It is time that we incorporate this mirroring connection between individuals and the group in all our explorations of human nature. It is also time we stop scapegoating the group (or the individual) when we encounter human characteristics that we find unacceptable. Jeffrey Burton Russell demonstrates this approach in an essay entitled "The Evil One":

> But what is happening when a society gives itself so completely over to evil? Are we simply adding up a large number of individual angers and evils, a lot of individual devils? Or is something more sinister and frightening actually happening? Social psychologists have long been investigating mob behavior, but it is fair to say that we still know a great deal more about its effects than about its mechanisms. Lewis Thomas and other biologists have pointed to the intense social behavior of other animals. Swarms of bees, for example, seem to act not so much like individual bees in a group as a large organism in which the bees have become functioning parts—we might almost say cells—of the whole. The swarm is in effect an organism. It seems to be able to act, even perhaps to decide, as a whole, communicating its collective will by mechanisms that we are just beginning to understand. Comparable behavior has been observed in human groups—in mobs particularly, but other groups as well—when individual wills seem to be submerged in the will of the whole. The behavior of the Nazi crowds at Nuremburg or of the Chinese Red Guards are notorious examples. (1988, pp. 55–56)

He goes on to answer his own questions:

> It seems improbable that adding up individual sins, even in large numbers, can produce something as appalling as the Nazi Holocaust. It seems more likely that a collective focus of evil is at work with its own agenda and purpose, a composite evil raised to a new dimension of intensity and malignity.

Let us go one step further. If, as Jung suggested, there is such a thing as a collective human unconscious—if humanity, in other words, is less a collection of individuals than something like an organic unity, then there may be a focus of evil, a malign force with its own will and agenda, operating within humanity as a whole. (Ibid.)

And, on the most positive side of the group mystery, here is a personal glimpse of what can be achieved by a collective at its most quintessential creative moments. I was at Symphony Hall in San Francisco listening to a performance of Bach's *St. Matthew's Passion*. I know the music well; I had been listening to recordings for many months in preparation for this live performance. I started out a member of the audience, but once the first double chorus began I was also on the stage, increasingly a part of the conductor, the musicians, the singers, the ensemble, and the soloists, as they played from Bach's incomparable score. Bach, too, was present, incredibly present. He awes, he pervades, and soon he is simply there, telling the sad and strange story of human sacrifice and redemption. Jesus was present, too, the Last Supper, Judas, Golgotha, Pilate, Barabbas, the Romans, and the Jews. Bach created much of this from inside himself. The music is so personal, and yet, as Albert Schweitzer said about Bach, "this genius was not an individual but a collective soul." So the collective soul of two thousand years was in the hall. I was aware of how well Bach accepted the collective and himself as part of the same fabric, how little he asked to dominate, how he gave each performer and each instrument its own way. This great piece of music, surely one of the greatest ever written, celebrated human sacrifice to the collective and the collective to the individual. As I listened, the ever-present observer marked a thought for the "mystery" chapter: Bach went far beyond this passion play, the story of a human sacrifice, and beyond Christianity, too, when he wrote this. And this performance went far beyond who we usually allow ourselves to be. This piece—its origins, its meaning, and its performance—is about harmony—the individual and the collective in harmony—and for a brief time I was a willing and coherent part of that vision.

4

Exploring the Group Mystery: The Organ of Group Consciousness

Depth psychology and depth analysts have described the ways the collective unconscious can be explored through the individual psyche and the therapeutic dyad. Exploring the collective psyche through the group is another portal, as anthropologists and sociologists have amply demonstrated.

But how can we, as psychologists, begin to explore the innards of a group's own experience, the mystery of the group, the experience of collective awareness as center point? For example, how do individuals and groups manage the phase shift from "I" to "we," the shifting boundaries of consciousness between individual and group? Can we learn to enhance group consciousness states for constructive and creative purposes as effectively as mob structures demonstrate its negative aspects? A more profound group consciousness is a goal in some meditations, as for example in the Buddhist practice of expanding one's awareness to embrace the suffering of others. In my own experience as a group consultant, I find that group consciousness is largely repressed by individualizing perceptions; it takes work to bring it to the foreground, just as it takes work to enter any "alternate" reality.

Group awareness, however, is only an "altered" state of consciousness if we define the "I" or ego-consciousness state as the only "natural" consciousness. After all, we speak, think, feel, and communicate emotions all in the language of a specific collective. As Sapir (1949) showed more than forty years ago, our grammar, derived from the collective, structures our concepts, our very way of thinking. We dream collective dreams. We "see" through our individual eyes, but also through group eyes, through class eyes, through ethnic eyes, and we "hear" through our group's language. Group consciousness is our continual reality, our delight and our fear. We are simply not well schooled in using it for our own benefit.

None of these manifestations of group consciousness are at odds with being an individual, for sensation, language, and meaning are also individual phenomena; one's individual consciousness and one's group consciousness intersect, sharing common ground with each other. It is our penchant for a narrowly defined individuality in opposition to the collective that constricts us, prevents us from grasping the whole, stops us short of the fullness of individuation.

A self-conscious focus on individuality is not our only birthright. It is not even our origin. We begin our consciousness in merger with another. In most cultures, developmental process moves the child from that state of merger toward individual separateness. In chapter 2, I discussed how our self-conscious individuality develops out of the earlier collective consciousness or, more accurately, out of the myriad dyads and groups in which we share and to which we belong. My investigation suggests that the child's individual consciousness grows out of, but does not supplant, his or her group-family consciousness, rather they continue to operate and evolve in tandem to each other as the individual develops. If we aggrandize individuality at the expense of the group, it is perhaps because as children we feel our individuality as a powerful achievement yet so fragile, delicate, and insubstantial. If we continue to feel the nature of our individual identity to be insubstantial into adulthood, then the group—that other part of consciousness—will indeed be perceived as dangerous rather than as a potential source of love, power, and creativity, as only an enemy and never a friend. Then the group will become an object on which we project our negative feelings, in which we reify the shadow, the mob, the regressive, abasing influence of the cult. Perhaps most poignantly, the group often becomes one place to project our fear of loss of that precious individuality.

All of this works against the individuation process, which requires the holding of polarities, including our individual and collective natures, as separate but intersecting parts. This, after all, is the really radical insight and methodology of depth psychology, and this reaffirms why depth psychology must include an exploration of collective psychology and extend the analytic exploration of the collective in the individual psyche from dreams and fantasy to actual group manifestations.

One way to proceed might be to postulate an organ of group consciousness, an organ connected but not identical to a part of us that is an organ of individual consciousness. One could say that this organ of collective consciousness is the heir to our "primitive" collectivity, our connection to other species—birds, herd animals, insects—for whom collective consciousness and collective altruism are directly linked to biological survival. To the human species, evolution has added the adventure of individual consciousness and its attendant emphasis on separateness and autonomy to the multitude of life's experiments, and thus far it has proved to be powerfully adaptive, much as flying has proved to be adaptive to birds and swimming to fish. But our enlarged cerebrum and its expanding neural pathways have also had important effects on group consciousness in the form of extraordinary developments in our collective structures—consciousness of species, nation, family, class, profession, friendship, and all the other groups that occupy and comprise our individual minds.

We tend to interpret these remarkable developments in human social evolution, particularly Western social evolution, as being in service to individual consciousness; developments in collective consciousness are most often viewed as serving to further individual development. "Success" in human affairs, as the Incas discovered when facing the Spaniards, has tended to go to the most highly individualized among us. But the adaptivity, and therefore the apparent primacy, of individual consciousness is now in question precisely because of the consequences of this success. Having given individuality and individual consciousness high value without continuing to emphasize our essential collective roots and relationships, we have achieved unprecedented domination on our planet and created a context of almost total unrelatedness to the other living systems with which we share our living space and on which we ultimately depend. Perhaps the development of individual consciousness in humans will turn out to be an evolutionary cul-de-sac, rendering us unsuited to harmonious relationship with species that do not share our potential for or obsession with individuality. Or perhaps we can recapture knowledge of and reverence for our human collectivity and its connections to other collectivities, perhaps without losing our individual nature.

To rephrase the question at the beginning of this chapter, how can we develop this organ of group consciousness and intensify our awareness of collectivity in the same way we have developed a deep awareness of our individuality? What would it mean to enhance our ability to see through the group's eyes as well as individual eyes, to move easily between individual and group realities, to experience the web and the spider simultaneously. There are many academic disciplines that concern human groups, but they rarely include in their exploration of collective consciousness the perspective of the unconscious. We do find some evidence of the unconscious in very diverse places: self-proclaimed psychics who feel their dreams are not personal but collective are working at this level. Prophets from every century—men and women who, like Jeremiah and Teresa of Ávila, give up their personal lives and personal visions for collective ones—are tapping the collective unconscious (Herschell 1962). So are the leaders, social and political, who place themselves in the maw and wellspring of the collective as well as inside their own skin. The symphony conductor and the basketball coach must work at this level to be successful, and so must great athletes in team sports and successful corporate executives. Likewise, group therapists, organizational consultants, and sociologists and theologians whose interest is the unconscious psychology of human groups and interaction between groups must become sensitive to collectivity.

Over the past twenty years, I have been intrigued by group consciousness as an "altered" state and have tried to heighten my consciousness of the collective experientially, especially with those collectives I have joined as a member or as a consultant. I consider my work as an organizational consultant as the authorization to explore the collective unconscious of a specific group, and I try to work only with client groups who accept this definition of my role and expect to benefit from such explorations. My clients have included businesses, educational and mental health institutions, boards of directors, and international political and psychological conferences. Along with my colleague Pilar Montero, who co-consults with me in some of the above enterprises, I also lead workshops on archetypes of the group, at the C. G. Jung Institute of San Francisco and elsewhere, which explore unconscious collective processes with groups formed for that purpose. These workshops are related, although not identical, to group relations conferences based on the Tavistock approach to groups, the focus of which is more on authority and leadership issues and less on the unconscious and archetypal nature of group life (Miller and Rice 1965). This work has deepened my apprehension about and appreciation of the collective unconscious in very specific group situations, and it has carried over to the way I experience the many other professional and friendship groups of which I am a part.

In chapter 6, I will describe the instrumental aspects of consulting in depth more directly. Here I want to focus on the subjective experience of this work, the shamanic-like "crossing over" from individual to group consciousness. Let me begin by describing my experience with a small group, a gathering of less than a dozen people, that had hired me to consult to their collective process.

I sit in a room in a circle of people whom I do not know well (or at all) as individuals. They could be the employees and owners of a small business, a professional group, a conference group, or the leaders of a community or profession. Whoever they are, they define themselves as a group and need or want to explore their own collective process for a variety of conscious and unconscious reasons. At many points during the day or days of sitting with them, I will need to make a comment on what I experience of this group, not to the individuals but to the group as a network of thoughts, feelings, interactions, and mergings. I have learned certain inner ways of aligning my mind's experience with this task.

The word *grok* comes to mind, that hunchlike apprehension of more than oneself that is so well described by Heinlein in his novel *Stranger in a Strange Land.* I wonder how Ted Sturgeon learned about triadic merger in *More Than Human* and how Ursula K. Le Guin grasped the ritual collaborative symbiosis of what she calls "foretelling" in *The Left Hand of Darkness.* Why is science fiction so often interested in the group merger states? My own development and work owe a great debt to this literary form. I read so much of it while I was in college, a parallel intellectual track to the assigned readings of individualistic philosophers of the classical, Renaissance, and Enlightenment eras. They always inspired me to continue with my own "fuzzier" interest in the experience of merger phenomena, including collective psychology, while pursuing a more traditional curriculum.

I do not edit these meanderings. They are a form of induction into my task, a way of letting go and "dissolving" into the group while watching the way this happens for clues about the psychology of the specific group I am among. To work in a group this way, I need to know the compound better than the molecules, and the mixture more than the compound. I must soften my focus and my boundaries, then expand my awareness to include the experience of myself in the group, then the group in me, and finally just the group. The pattern of the whole must emerge full force. In temporarily accepting the group collective as my consciousness, I must trust that the "I" will be back later to translate what I have experienced into the language of individuality so that I can communicate it. But for now, I am reaching toward an "other side" of consciousness.

The induction is critical to the balance I want between collective experience and individual memory; and like all beginnings, it holds the seeds of all that I will learn. In some groups, I can let go of the strong "I" and descend into the maw of the others while my collective organ feels its way unhampered into the patterned psyche of the group. But this is rare; only experienced groups of fairly comfortable individuals who are used to this collective focus will facilitate such a change of state so unselfconsciously and undefensively. More often, my collective stance inspires anxiety, for no matter what the initial contract, no matter how seriously concerned all the individuals present are about their group's fate, few of them can feel comfortable when the group identity and process are paramount, when they as individuals go unnamed and unrecognized.

When there is anxiety and resistance to my collective stance, there is also more friction at the boundary, and the induction has a more searing quality. It is difficult to let the initial group images wash over me, to accept the group's thoughts and feelings as my own, and to allow fantasies to grow out of group projections, their incarnation of me. But difficult or not, I must leave part of my ego behind in order to enter the group's collective self. As I do so, as I feel the group more and more and me less and less, my experience becomes dreamlike, a dream in which there is no "I" present that is more powerful than any of the other characters and plots and feelings of the "we." But always there is an observer, a witness somewhere in a neutral corner, feeling, seeing, remembering, and preserving the experience until the "I" awakes, much as a dream is felt, seen, remembered, and preserved. It is the presence of this witness that lets me let go into the "we," enter the interactive dance, the rush of intermingling feeling, the rhythms and music of speech, the drumbeat of dialogue, the syncopating pause of silence. Collective consciousness is a symphonic experience: solos, duets, sections, and finally the whole. It is bodies, too, breathing, smells, intimate connections. It is all this and also a single throbbing entity which includes my consciousness and others' consciousness, but also always the ensemble, the One.

As groups become larger, the experience of consulting changes. Large groups create more anxiety among their members than small groups; individual identities are more powerfully diffused; individual differences are all but lost. Subjectively, the large-group consulting experience is an overwhelming feast of images and feelings, like wandering into a Casbah or ghetto without knowledge of language or customs. In such a situation, it is extremely difficult to use the tools necessary for collective exploration, to give up one's individual consciousness and allow the organ of group consciousness to hold sway. Arming oneself against the onslaught of the group unconscious through strict attention to professional role and boundaries is almost inevitable, and consulting from such a restricted perspective is difficult and uncreative, which further increases the hostility of the group.

In large-group situations, stereotyping according to superficial characteristics (such as skin color, age, gender, religion, and social class) and to large role and authority differences is an easier way to establish order and reason than sorting out differences and competencies. The consultant may need to point out such destructive mechanisms, which will inevitably engender more resistance. If the consultant works at such issues without trust or leverage, he or she may experience firsthand the most destructive aspect of large-group dynamics—scapegoating. I have found that consulting alone to a large group is a very risky affair. I have often found myself isolated for what appeared to me to be very simple statements about a seemingly obvious large-group dynamic. Even assigning collective responsibility within an amorphous system is threatening to many individuals.

Large groups can sometimes become unruly and dangerous mobs. That is one reason why even organizations that purport to study group life tend to shy away from the large-group explorations. Yet large groups all too frequently dominate our political structures and therefore our lives. Unless we believe that large groups are pure evil, we have to acknowledge that they, too, like all elements of the collective psyche, must contain positive as well as negative potential, and we must learn how to explore and develop the positive potential just as dictators and demagogues have learned how to develop the negative potential.

I personally find consulting to large groups among my most meaningful and mysterious activities in the group arena. They hold the full power of the group archetype and the collective psyche, an awesome dynamo, without the insulation that face-to-face interaction in smaller groups provides. The issues of small groups are like fairy tales, the extension of family and school life; they are far less intense compared to the mythic dramas played out in the large-group collective. The large group is about extremes and intensity: suffering and joy, stagnation and ecstasy, cosmic space and the black hole, and also about the fantastic fullness of the human psyche, for within the large group the total human condition is played out.

When I consult to a large group, I try to set conditions that will allow the full play of these forces in as secure a psychic space as possible, and working as a team is an important element here. Usually I try to work with one experienced partner with whom I have already developed a close and trusting relationship. A close working relationship with a fellow consultant provides enough security to remain in role without diminishing the symbolic space available to that role. For similar reasons, I try whenever possible to create a consulting duo which enhances diversity along the lines of age, gender, or race and which mirrors some basic characteristic of the large group with whom I am working. (Adding additional representative consultants may be helpful, although more than three or four creates the further complication of another group to be understood and experienced.) The absence of a woman consultant in a large group with many women members inevitably focuses the group on issues of male domination, the abuse and disenfranchisement of women, and the absence of the feminine—all meaningful cultural issues, but ones which are usually cooling diversions from the heat of the collective psyche of that particular group. A similar pattern emerges if there is no person of color on the consulting team to a multiracial group. This is not to say that such issues may not be present in the group, only that they can be ideological scapegoats imported through the personae of the consultants which hide the deeper issues and ultimately the deeper mysteries of a particular group.

As the discussion above suggests, large groups are symbolic transformers: everything one does takes on mythic proportions beyond the personal thought, feeling, or action. Even the decision to enter the large group with a small preformed team of working colleagues organized ahead of time is felt to incarnate the mysteries associated with all powerful intrusions, including impregnation. In the psychic space of the large group, the act of beginning a consultation almost inevitably constellates the twin mysteries of sex and procreation. The consultants bring their probing light into a dark and chaotic world, and the union of these forces presages a hopeful new order in the form of a divine child, or a monstrous miscarriage. In fact, a large group will constellate both divine child and monstrous miscarriage; both will be represented, and both need to be explored and tolerated or the group will never fully accept the reality of the collective psyche and the reality of the consultant's task.

The process of consulting to a group is a series of such episodes; archetypal images are the stock in trade. The consultants, because they are so visible and also because they represent such a special function, often receive the brunt of the projections, particularly until the group members themselves are able to emerge from the protective background that large-group anonymity provides. The experience of consulting as a male-female pair is to feel powerfully drawn into highly emotional and evocative images such as King/Queen, Sun/Moon, Brother/Sister, and other archetypal representations of dyadic phenomena in the human unconscious. The experience of consulting as a trio is to know from the inside out the images of Oedipus, Jocasta, and Laius; of Father, Son, and Holy Ghost; of Husband, Wife, and Lover; and other variations of the human triangle. I am emphasizing the consultants' experience here because there is nothing abstract about being part of the projective field of a large group searching for a way out of chaos and confusion. The field evokes and incarnates; it is lived out by the group until, often through consultation, the ordering value of an old image is diminished and a new image takes its place. The progression of these images in time takes on symbolic significance of its own; a story fragment emerges, then an entire story, and eventually a myth with the power to capture enough unique elements of the group to give its life meaning. Elements of the myth may be played out in different parts of the group and the themes repeated in cycles until there is a sense of the large group as small society, telling and retelling its origin, its history, its laws, its values and ethics, and even predicting its future.

The consultant familiar with the way the unconscious processes symbols—for example, the polarization of images and feelings and the transformation of image and feelings through complexes into stories and myths which have numinous impact—will, if fear of these powerful unconscious processes can be stilled, be as much at home in the large group as in a dream. It is an immersion in the kind of unconscious experience that is activated in a working analysis or a psychedelic drug experience or one of the many other states in which the objective psyche is apprehended more or less directly. But fear of the group functions like a powerful repressing drive; like the fear of a nightmare to an insomniac, it is the fear of being overwhelmed by unconscious forces, forces that both are and aren't one's own, that are both in and beyond one's control. When one is totally immersed in a nightmare, the fear is absolute, while in the group, although there is rarely the same degree of loss of ego identity, the possibility of "real" destruction is far greater, the combination more than enough for an ego that fears total immersion and fights against it. To work in the unconscious without fear taking over—for example, in analysis, a drug experience, or even a dream—is to accept, with whatever observing ego is available, that the emerging images and feelings, even when temporarily negative and threatening, will inevitably be balanced from the positive side. Sometimes, when there is enough observing ego in the dreamer and the dream is frightening enough, it is possible, even essential, to will oneself awake from the nightmare. Likewise in a group, it may be necessary to try to alter dramatically the course of the group's process through action or interpretation in order to avert disaster. But most of the time, fear-inspired action in a group is mirrored in the unconscious collective drama with a fear-inspiring process, such as scapegoating.

In my experience, it is the lack of appreciation for the unconscious collective at work that throws a group into a frenzy and activates the fear-inspired abasement that Jung so abhors. This is not to imply that large groups are not dangerous; groups are embodied dreams with blood-and-guts consequences for all participants, but they are also highly creative spaces. They are capable of precipitating truly remarkable, if unstable, transformations in individuals, in ideas, in whole nations. I have never left a large group without a sense of both wariness and awe toward the human collective at work.

The process of crossing over into group consciousness shares much with crossing over into other "altered" states. The common element is the initial loss of "I," the ego, and the characteristic reaction of a mixture of anxiety and ecstasy. In the crossing over to group consciousness, there is no need for candle flame, mantra, or drug as catalyst. The group's psyche is quite enough, for it diffuses the "I" by activating one's organ of group consciousness, one's collective nature—one's sentience and connectedness. After the initial breakthrough, after the "white light" that seems to be a universal part of one's first brush with deindividualization states, patterns develop from the fantasies, visions, and myths that make up our unconscious collective.

To become suddenly connected to the upwelling of potent and unfamiliar imagery in a group is an awesome experience and one that will frighten many individuals and subgroups. One's effectiveness as a consultant depends on staying open to the fragments of group images and feelings even when they are unpleasant or painful, for they are the channel of access to the unconscious of the group. To allow these collective images to coalesce and crystallize is to experience a set of related stories emerging, to become enveloped by strange and wonderful myths woven out of the fabric of the ongoing group process. These myths feel as if they begin far below the surface of each individual's consciousness, from a place in which a more common consciousness directs the group psyche. They function experientially to organize the anxiety of the loss of "I," but far more importantly, they embody the ecstatic inchoateness of the "non-I" experience we share. With patience, these threads and bits of stories, each holding some piece of the group, intersecting and intermingling with one another, knit together to make a coherent whole. As this happens, there is a noticeable lessening of anxiety as meaning is given to the common experience.

To the observer-witness in the neutral corner, the consultant-in-waiting, the patterning of the group's experience is a step out of chaos toward coherence. Meaningful images awaken the observer and activate the consultant role, and the struggle to connect image to words and metaphor begins. In a sense, one's "I" reemerges from the group dream to become group storyteller, the one who will give words, images, and emotions to the collective myth.

It has been wisely said that any meaningful interpretation in psychotherapy is also experienced as a loss. This is because a familiar (if neurotic) structure has been undermined. What the unconscious provides in response is new and often frightening. The same is true of group interpretations, including a good story. Consulting to a group involves uncovering a process which inexorably links the individuals to their collective myth with the consultant as group storyteller. This is almost always experienced as a painful surprise to individuals who have previously felt themselves to be independent actors in the group drama. They now experience an essential duality: individuality is also collectivity. Suddenly the woven web *is* as important as the spinning spider. Some individuals experience this insight as a loss: the group reality is felt to be diminishing and abasing with no additional redeeming value from the newfound connection to the collective. For others, the added dimension of experience adds depth, another mysterious world to be fathomed, one that transcends individual awareness. A skillful consultant leads the group members toward their secrets in a way that enhances the mystery and meaning without activating too much loss and anger.

The consultant is not the only "witness" in the group; individual members may also see their behavior as simultaneous products of the individual and collective dramas. Many group members do this at times, but generally it is extremely difficult for engaged participants to experience both levels of meaning simultaneously. Group members are far more caught up in the unconscious matrix than a consultant whose role is to engage only for the purpose of exploring the matrix with them. Where I find the most difficulty is not so much in capturing the group consciousness but in translating it back across the boundary to the individuals. I experience constraint in my consultation when I empathize too strongly with the individuals involved; I do best in telling the group its story when I am not too burdened by the temporarily hurt feelings of any given group members. However, I also need the empathy in order to tell the group story in ways that individuals as well as the collective can hear and use. When I do speak well, when I have caught something of the collective awareness and found a poignant image with which to capture it, even the most threatened individuals listen. If a chord is struck, the collective vibrates deep within the group and what was said is not only oracular madness—there is always some of that in any good group interpretation—but also a new level of collective meaning and strengthened relationship with the group unconscious.

Because I am a well-known consultant and am paid to provide group interpretations, the group usually provides a grace period, like a new president's one hundred days, during which they suspend their natural apprehensions about interpretations at the level of the unconscious collective. A continuing relationship with the group's unconscious depends on engendering a trustworthy dialogue between group interpretation and individual experience. Group members need to begin to join me in understanding the myths and images as group phenomena. As the consultation continues, the group's collective unconscious

71

begins to talk through its individual members. Each of us becomes actor and sibyl, learning how to honor the experiences of individuality and collectivity and to comment on both.

Group work of this kind can be understood as a special form of meditation, a meditation in which one's relation to the collective is the central focus. Many forms of meditation use the group as a starting place to facilitate the loosening of ego boundaries. As meditation deepens, consciousness of oneself in the group, oneself in the human collective, is often taken as a way station on the road to a more abstracted sense of oneness. Most methods of meditation teach that the rich imagery so prominent in the identification with the collective psyche consists of "karmic" or "bardo" visions to be put aside as distractions. From the perspective of group consultation, the quest for more abstracted states of consciousness becomes a temptation away from the continuing relation to the group and a deepening connection to the human collective. In the course of consulting to a group, I often find myself moving along such a path, and so do many group members as they begin to experience a stronger connection with the collective unconscious. It is tempting to move from individual to universal, from a loss of ego to the great void. How grand to merge with the cosmos; how mundane and difficult to merge with our fellow humans.

One important reason for this difficulty is the issue of collective responsibility. Most individuals find collective responsibility even more threatening than individual responsibility. The scapegoat is, after all, a most powerful collective archetype. There always seems to be more to gain by blaming others than by accepting our fundamental role in what others do. We do not want to become more conscious of our interdependence; we all have enough pain of our own as individuals. All of us are expert at projecting our own pain onto the group and then distancing ourselves from that pain by denying our membership, our collective responsibility. Here individual analysis and depth consultation become syntonic, parallel forms, where the individual and the group are mirrors of one another, made of the same stuff— us. Both activities teach about the essential connectedness of hero and shadow, of messiah and scapegoat. One of the lessons we have learned from the individual psyche is that only by accepting and, if necessary, exploring the wound will we increase our understanding and further our development.

We are now only beginning to accept that this premise applies to groups as well. Externalized solutions in the form of economic expansion, the acquisition of new technology, finding an outside enemy, or developing an inner enemy, a scapegoat, have been the traditional and successful alternatives to self-examination within the group. Colonialism, war, exploitative economics, and political structures based on class, race, and gender—all variations on the theme of scapegoating—are still our favorite ways of solving large-scale collective problems, and smaller groups and organizations follow this lead. Study of the group itself is rarely considered an alternative, even when the damage of not doing so is great. Calling on a consultant gives a group the chance to explore and eventually change damaging processes, much as analysis provides this opportunity to individuals. Unfortunately, even when the consultant is welcomed into a group or organization, and even though an adequate consulting alliance seems to be developing, the strong tendency is to blame individuals or see solutions within individuals, blame abstractions or see the solutions in abstractions, rather than centering on the collective process itself.

From the point of view of the group, it is obvious why the consultant poses a threat, for just as the individual sees the impersonal group as a danger to his or her development, so the group, taken as a unit, sees the unaffiliated and unsocialized individual—in this case, the consultant—as a danger to its status quo. It is here, from within the group, that the individual's sense of abasement originates, for when threatened—either from outside by real or projected economic, social, or political forces, or from inside by the interpretation of the consultant—the group defends itself from the individual causing the trouble by attempting to civilize the person or, if that fails, by imprisoning, expelling, or otherwise nullifying his or her presence. The consultant in the group, like the analyst in the dyad, is always challenging the customary way of accomplishing the work, always pushing at the boundaries of definitions and assumptions.

Even though the consultant has been consciously hired to perform this task, the group unconscious will deal with this threat by pigeonholing the consultant into a role in which he or she is symbolically destroyed. This is akin to the way a patient develops a transference toward the analyst as a way of stabilizing a past known relationship instead of honoring a new relationship devoted to change and growth. As we know from analysis, the seeds of real change are encoded in that transference, in the sequential re-creation and transformation of the old relationship. Unlocking that code requires interpretation of the transference in an atmosphere of safety. In the individual analytic situation, there is the potential to form the transference gradually and hone the accuracy of interpretation through conscious and unconscious feedback. But while the same encoding process is necessary in the transference to the group consultant, it is far more difficult to develop a safe and trusting container. There is rarely enough time to develop and refine interpretations and there is always a potential scapegoat for the undeveloped, uncommitted group to blame. Failing all else, the consultant is a ready-made scapegoat, perfectly positioned to be cast as the cause of rather than the cure for a group's problems. As uncomfortable as this may become for the consultant, accepting the scapegoat role consciously by interpreting to the group this blatantly self-defeating dynamic may be the beginning of a serious exploration of the deeper aspects of the group's collective world.

The interpretive process in consulting from within a collective consciousness and to a group is, paradoxically, also highly personal. There is no way to gain objective accuracy or interpretative validity in such work, any more than this can be achieved in other subjective realms such as the dyad of analysis. Even as I cross and recross the boundary between individual and group consciousness, I bring along my own subjectivity, my own language, my own set of symbols, and my own complexes. The stories that I hear and the interpretations that I make are filtered through my individual and collective experience. Yet it is this very personal intensity in a consultation that opens up an interstitial dimension for the group in which a new kind of symbolic language can be spoken, turning on the lights on a previously darkened tableau.

A fellow consultant, working together with me in a large group, had a dream which beautifully captured this dimension of group consultation. In the dream, I was a harlequin figure, beautiful and dangerous, who entered a large, mysterious house carrying a glowing lantern and went from one darkened room to another. In each room were still figures, beasts and angels, which the light from my lantern brought to life. I visited each room, activating each small world, until the entire mansion was a carnival of activity, brimming with dance, music, and story as the mysterious beasts and angels created their own unique tableaux together.

The dream captured the essence of the explorative process in working with this large group. Each journey into the group mind, each comment on what we envisioned in that web, increased the group's symbolic space, bringing more and more light to the unconscious processes of our group. When we began, the space was dark and the rooms full of shadows. As we worked in our consulting pair and were joined by group members in that work, the space filled with life and the "beasts and angels" came alive.

This sense of entering an already existing interstitial space, a potentially symbolic space, and "turning on the lights" by crossing the threshold to the "other" world of group consciousness, is captured in Henry Corbin's term *mundus imaginalis* (1975). Montero describes this perspective as "taking the connecting medium for granted. It is a perspective which proposes that people who enter into relationship are already united: it is the very air they breathe. They immediately have shared images because the images and the structures that connect the images, the stories and the myths, are already there—enfolding, effecting, being" (1992, p. 205).

The consulting process I am describing requires ongoing work on developing the organ of group consciousness, continually extending the focus of psychological inquiry beyond the individual or the dyad to the group. Here we enter areas of experience variously called the imaginal, the shamanic realm, or the collective unconscious. Although I have spent many years training individuals to develop competence in this way of working, I still find it difficult to predict who will excel. Professional interest can be misleading. Therapists are trained to recognize unconscious process but are often uncomfortable with extending their field of inquiry beyond the individual or dyad, while organizational consultants appreciate the systems concept but their necessary pragmatism often conflicts with entering the more mysterious realms of the group. More relevant is a personal interest and experience with altered states of consciousness, particularly those with more extroverted expressions. Another common characteristic is comfort with living at the boundary of social units; many of the best consultants share a history of feeling peripheral (although not excluded) from their own families of origin and their peer groups. Being able to function within this boundary role is often described as being critical to their psychological survival when they were children. Most recently, many more individuals have been interested in learning this non-individual-centered perspective, perhaps as a response to the ecological movement's stress on interdependence. However, interdependence as an abstraction is a very different matter from joining minds and sharing imaginal realms together. Still, loosening the ideological boundaries of individualism helps all of us to work on developing a mode of consciousness which emphasizes our potential for a deep sentience and communion within the small and large groups in which we live and on whom we depend.

5

The Language of the Group: Stories, Myths, and Archetypes

THE ACT OF EXPLORING THE UNCONSCIOUS COLLECTIVE IN A group creates the need for a special language. If one views the group as a collection of individuals, the task of finding meaning among the complexities of group interactions becomes somewhat daunting. There is little possibility of carrying out the kind of careful, minute analysis of feeling, relationship, or dream that takes place in individual therapy or self-study. Instead, the consultant and participants search for generalization, moving toward larger themes and more-encompassing images that take in the whole of the group and provide a semblance of shared meaning to individual members. Sometimes this tendency leads toward superficial and stereotyped statements which denigrate the creations of the group. But when it is successful, the search for overarching themes and concepts can lead to interpretations that transform seemingly random, individual acts into meaningful patterns of behavior. This is the language of the feeling-laden image, the powerful teaching story, the myth that provides connection and meaning to the group as a whole by transcending the seemingly separate contributions of individual members.

From the perspective of the collective, then, the language of the group is story and myth, either because this is the way that groups speak or because it is the way that individuals can comprehend the group through language. Either way, it is the language of collective consciousness. Artists speak in such terms, and so do visionary leaders. When, in my role as group consultant, I am working well, I speak from the organ of group consciousness as a group storyteller and myth maker. The experience is one of being a kaleidoscope of plots, images, and music, all gradually sifting into the collecting vessel of a myth large enough to give meaning to the patterns. Consulting this way is an amazingly complex and rich experience, like being in many plays simultaneously, whose meaning I must grasp long enough to share with its creator, the group.

Sometimes this group story begins in a central image which captures and unifies what otherwise feels like a chaotic system, the *mundus imaginalis* in action. As an example, Montero describes a request for consultation to a therapy training institute in crisis because of a sexual relationship between a well-known analyst and his analysand, a candidate in training at the institute (Montero 1992). In her consultation, she used the image of Chinnamasta, a Hindu goddess, standing naked and decapitated and bleeding on the back of a copulating couple as a way of describing the archetypal basis of the organizational crisis. The interpretation was profoundly unpopular. It implied a larger issue than a single ethical violation by a disturbed analyst and a more complicated solution than simply kicking out the offending analyst. The image of the institute as the naked, decapitated, and bleeding goddess aroused the imagination of this analytic community and led it to explore its own scapegoating processes and the shadow behavior that scapegoating obscured. Montero describes the outcome as follows:

> The force inherent in an image such as that of Chinnamasta is so great it sparks the *mundus imaginalis* into play. Immediately, I want to warn the institute not to cap the geyser of fresh blood or disperse its flow so that the goddess and the devotees are no longer nourished by it. This fountain of imaginal possibilities is the life supply which can arise from those wounded, monstrous, freakish parts that lead us

to the archetypal base of life, the soul matrix, from whence new possibilities arise and old ones are reshaped. It would be tragic to seal over what has been activated with more professional persona resembling a miniaturized facsimile of the governance and adversarial judicial systems of the nation and their obvious deficits. It is an opportunity for the place to fertilize its understanding of analytical work, reassess its mission and realign its structure to match better the needs and trappings of analysts and their work. For example, a chairman and his advisory group, or a pair of leaders, or a troika, could be considered as a model for governance different from the typical president–vice president form. But more significant is the opportunity now available for people to reconnect with the sacred and give it its due place at the center and to stop treating archetypal events only as lodged inside individuals who are bad or sick and need to be punished or cured. (1992, p. 222)

Montero's goddess image for the institute in crisis was a freeze-frame of the enfolding larger story or myth which a community embodies. Bringing such a story to consciousness may or may not significantly alter the course of the story, but it does give meaning to an experience that would remain otherwise quite unconscious to the participants. Meaning itself may allow the group to embody their myth on a symbolic level and thus forestall actions such as scapegoating that do not serve the future development of the group.

Each group has its own story to live out, just as individuals have their stories to live out; the group's story is separate from, although related to, the stories of the individual members of the group. The individual's story is often couched in terms of a single archetype, most often the Hero, and most hero myths portray the struggle of the individual to sever his or her negative connection to the collective, often symbolized as the Great Mother. Hero myths are important incidents in the larger tableaux of group myths, epochs in which one or more heroes carry the energy of transformation for an entire collective. The Bible, *The Kalevala*, the *Ramayana*, the *Iliad*, the Arthurian legends, Shakespeare's history plays, Tolkien's Trilogy of the Ring, Asimov's *Foundation*—many of the great works of literature are stories tracing the development of families, clans, tribes, nations, or whole galaxies as entities in themselves. Historians tell us these stories in their scholarly tradition and historical novelists in theirs. The stories are also the concern of the great psychologists whose particular genius was in transforming their individual analytic cases into mythic journeys anchored in the collective. So Freud's great collective myth was Sophocles' *Oedipus Rex,* on which he based his theory of the unconscious structure of the family, and Jung joined individual psychology and world mythology through the postulation of a collective unconscious. From the opposite perspective, Bion's "basic assumptions" of group life—dependency, fight-flight, and pairing—were unconscious meta-stories which helped explain the effects of the group mind on the individual's psychology (Bion 1959).

Ultimately the distinctions between "individual" and "group" myth are only technical aids in understanding complex human processes. We focus our attention on one or another element of a polarity, such as individual or group, as it serves meaning to a particular moment in our life cycles or cultural development. When I work as an analyst, I focus on the person finding his or her "story"; the group is a background for the individuation process. When I work as a group consultant, it is the group story and the development of the collective to which I attend. From this perspective, for example, the great Arthurian legends are less a series of questing hero myths and more a myth of male group utopia, symbolized by the Round Table, in which a brotherhood of equals collaborate in the pursuit of truth and social justice.

The way groups learn and grow is mirrored in the myths they embody. Three central group myths—the scapegoat, the island, and the Round Table—taken together, describe a widespread developmental sequence of group and societal maturation.

The first myth in the sequence is that of the scapegoat and its Janus twin, the myth of the messiah. As discussed in chapter 1, the scapegoat is the most pervasive myth of group life. It underlies the shaky stability of human collective life; it dominates our justifications for war through the concept of the enemy and for social inequality through the concept of the underling and the structures of social class. It is a powerful force in most of our religious, educational, work, and family systems as well. Christianity is based on the scapegoat/messiah myth; Islam uses the infidel and the Jihad as two of its sustaining pillars; and Judaism has the chosen people as its central concept. In modern life, scapegoating is the root of major social issues on the campus and in the workplace—sexism and racism. It is part of a basic family pattern which creates abused and victimized children who later become abusing and victimizing parents. These patterns with which we now take issue are not new; they are the more recent manifestations of a scapegoating process that goes back to human sacrifice.

The basis of the scapegoat myth is this: the group is not to blame for its problems, its bad feelings, its pain, its defeats. These are the responsibility of a particular individual or subgroup—the scapegoat—who is perceived as being fundamentally different from the rest of the group and must be excluded or sacrificed in order for the group to survive and remain whole.

One way to understand this phenomenon is to appreciate the important psychological connections between the roles of the scapegoat in the group and the shadow in the individual. Just as the individual uses unconscious mechanisms to detoxify and reject the shadow elements from consciousness, so the group uses scapegoating to detoxify and reject negative elements from its consciousness. It also follows that just as there is little individual development without facing the problem of one's shadow, there is little group development without facing the problem of the group's scapegoats. Thus, working through and past the scapegoating mechanism is almost always a necessary prelude to achieving a level of group development in which diversity and collective responsibility are encouraged. Once the group no longer focuses on saviors, heroes, victims, and enemies but on the contribution of each group member to the collective and the collective to each member, it enters a new level of development.

One common development beyond the scapegoat phase is a dynamic of isolation captured in the group myth of the island. The story line depends on the notion that the island is strong and self-sufficient, capable of controlling its own destiny without outside help. It is a group whose strength depends on internal cohesion as well as homogeneity. Island communities also recognize and even foster the development of difference within the community, but their survival depends on marshaling these inner resources and integrating them into the island collective rather than ever relying on the outside world.

The island ethos says: "We handle our own problems. We'll

mind our business. You mind yours." Scapegoating as a mechanism is still a potential in such collectives. The exclusionary stance of the island group carries with it a potential for paranoia—when threatened, the outside world, previously either neutral or ignored, quickly becomes the enemy, a return to the projective mechanisms of scapegoat mentality. The island dynamic works against this potential in that these collectives go out of their way to integrate shadow elements inside their boundaries. The resulting solutions are couched in terms of the good and welfare of the whole community.

The island myth is pervasive in the well-ordered middle class of the Western world. It underlies the assumption of self-sufficiency of nations like Switzerland, the small towns in midwestern America, and the walled communities of well-to-do urban and suburban enclaves across the world. It informs the many corporations who value independence over interdependence. In such collectives, disability, illness, and even antisocial behavior are tolerated as long as they can be viewed as "family" or "insider" problems. For example, many organizations have learned to provide extremely progressive and expensive rehabilitation programs for their employees while lobbying against similar benefits in outside groups. Similarly, a retarded child or a schizophrenic adult who "belongs" to a community may be allowed to garner valuable resources devoted to his or her integration and treatment, while those with the same problem but viewed as "outsiders," such as mentally ill homeless people, are treated as subhumans.

The island myth also underlies many authoritarian political structures and different kinds of cults; it is the ethos for fundamentalist communities and nations. And it is most effective as a guiding myth if the social unit is wealthy in the sense of containing most of its necessary resources within its boundaries. It often sees itself as creating its own self-sufficiency, but it is blind to the crucial contribution of hidden and liminal shadow elements such as untouchables and slaves.

Beyond this dehumanizing flaw, a fundamental problem for this kind of societal myth is exactly its isolationism. In our modern world, this means isolation from changing technology and cultural diversity—from new ideas and resources. Isolation in the collective eventually limits the sense of unbounded imagination, unlimited vistas, and the excitement of collaboration with others. There is no room within this mythology for the embodiment of the transcendent function, for mythic boundary-crossers inspired by the likes of Prometheus, Hermes, Dionysus, Coyote, and Loki. But, as John Donne said, "No man is an island," and neither is the human group for very long. The political events of the early 1990s in the former Soviet Union and Eastern Europe have demonstrated that island communities either regress into repetitive scapegoating to rid themselves of the differences they cannot encompass or are forced to open their boundaries to the outside world and undergo the inevitable and painful transformations to new forms of group development.

Such new forms of group development are still sadly lacking; realistically, there have been few human social and political systems that have endured without relying on scapegoating or isolation as major bulwarks to survival. Even unthreatened groups and groups with almost unlimited resources that have theoretically had more chance to develop collectives which contain diversity (the United States, for example) have relied on both isolation and scapegoating as stabilizing forces at various times and places throughout their histories. The former Soviet Union promulgated a myth that was supposed to go beyond scapegoating and in which isolation was a temporary phase until the rest of the world joined in its vision. We know now that scapegoating in the form of mass murders of dissident groups fueled that society. The democracies of the twentieth century have been supported by powerful scapegoating in the forms of racism and sexism or island mentalities for which homogeneity was a strict requirement. Humanity is still in evolutionary infancy; our ability to kill our own kind even when our survival is not clearly threatened is a glaring example of the aggressive, primitive level of group development in comparison to apparently "less developed" species. Just as infant humans need to exclude and consolidate as part of their identity development, so young groups may need to exclude through scapegoating and consolidate through isolation preliminary to further group development. In other words, scapegoating groups may give way to the more contained island groups as a part of the developmental process, and island groups must risk integrating both unwanted outsiders and alien others in order to progress.

Of the many utopian visions that society has dreamed about, all deal with these issues of integration, issues of sentience and service that increasingly include not just the variety found within our own species but the entire earth ecology. I personally find the vision of King Arthur's Round Table to be most compelling for its combination of interactively authorized leadership and deeply felt group responsibility and connectedness, as well as its commitment to serve not only Table members but the collective as a whole, a commitment to both task and process which serves both individual and collective psyche. One description of its beginnings is as follows:

> Arthur never heard speak of a knight in praise, but he caused him to be numbered of his household. Because of these noble lords about his hall, of whom each knight pained himself to be the hardiest champion, and none would count him the least praiseworthy, Arthur made the Round Table. . . . It was ordained of Arthur that when his fair fellowship sat to meat their chairs should be high alike, their service equal, and none before or after his comrade. Thus no man could boast that he was exalted above his fellow, for all alike were gathered round the bard, and none was alien at the breaking of Arthur's bread. (Matthews 1989, p. 27)

Arthur is the valued and authorized leader with a powerful mission, but he is not the wisest or the strongest of the group. He is not even the greatest hero, a designation which falls sequentially to many different knights, depending on the task at hand.

In the legends, the Round Table is a gift to Arthur and Guinevere by Merlin on the occasion of their marriage. Merlin says the table is to be "in the likeness of the world." The table symbolizes the induction of a new societal Self, a new world order, brought about by emphasizing the conjunction of difference—youth and age, various nationalities and talents—through a physical form that symbolized social and spiritual equality. At the center of Camelot was the principle of political equality. Arthur the king was not the authoritarian ruler but first among equals. Merlin institutionalized this principle by insisting on a collective task which would emphasize service for the good of the whole rather than heroics for the good of the one. Here is one rendition of the oath that was sworn by the knights in pursuit of this principle:

> Never to do outrage nor murder, and always to flee treason, also by no means to be cruel, but to give mercy unto him that asketh mercy . . . Also, that no man take on battles in a wrongful quarrel for no law, nor for worlds goods. (Matthews 1989, p. 30)

The Round Table is clearly a mirror of the society from which it has emerged and is not free from prejudice, including sexism and classism. Nor does it adequately contain that great human shadow, incest and incestuous violence. The foibles of humanity are not overcome in Camelot, but the vision is none-theless a profound one—a commitment to the task of serving both individual and collective. These ideals of medieval chivalry, incorporated into a unique structure which fostered both the knights' and the fellowship's development through a profound commitment to difference and connection, created a vision which is still unrealized in our times. It and other visionary myths in our collective unconscious continue to inspire change toward more inclusive forms of group and political development.

The developmental sequence I have outlined above—from scapegoating groups to island groups and finally to groups that begin to embody an ethos such as that of Arthur's Round Table—is present in microcosm in many groups as they mature and grow. Returning to the examples of the group worlds of the scientists and the candidates in chapter 3, it is striking how the myth of the scapegoat/messiah dominated both groups' functioning. The scientists had a clearly defined scapegoat/messiah in their previous leader, who was widely viewed as having sacrificed himself to serve the common good. Under his protection, individual efforts thrived; when he was gone, they faltered as if his presence and power had somehow held the dark forces of incompetence and irrationality at bay. When further emphasis on the individual, reflected in the choice of a new leader, did not stem the downhill course of the institute, some of the scientists viewed their collective structure as the problem, the "thing to fix" so that the individuals could get on with their work. I was called in to "fix" the collective. If I had naively accepted such a role, it is likely that I would have become either the next savior if I succeeded or the next scapegoat if I failed. Instead I renegotiated my role to symbolize the potential for change and growth within their collective in hopes that the scientists might be supported in redefining their roles in a comparable way. As they began to move toward an ethos which included collective development, change emerged from within their web of relationships rather than from outside in the person of the consultant or another new leader. In the course of the consultation, this emphasis on inner coherence and its potential for finding creative solutions, one form of the island myth, bore fruit. As we worked together, other collective structures and attendant myths took hold. The Round Table myth was particularly interesting for the scientists, given their commitment to the quest for an abstract truth rooted in very real, physical solutions.

The candidates were somewhat more conscious than the scientists about the importance of the collective process, and the danger of scapegoating individuals within it. They venerated the institute as a whole and were committed to its central value, depth analysis, but their allegiance was to the abstraction of the institute and they shrank from the actual group process, particularly when it threatened individual boundaries and the primacy of analysis. When their experience of the actual collective no longer lived up to their fantasies and idealizations, they turned it into a villain with the power to ruin their personal experiences as candidates. With the tacit acceptance of the members themselves, they had turned the collective itself into a scapegoat. As long as the emphasis on individual development had no counterweight in a commitment to the collective, the candidates and the institute as a whole remained dominated by the unconscious dynamics of a scapegoating community.

It was therefore not surprising to find a victim psychology and some real scapegoating among the members as well. The candidate structure was powerfully affected by the institute and its members, who had fashioned an organization that prided itself on its self-sufficiency and self-reliance. Recently, the institute faced a major ethical crisis which focused on sexually inappropriate behavior between an analyst and analysand who was also a candidate. As might be expected, the organization closed ranks around the scandal in an attempt to limit damage to the reputation of the training program and the institute as a whole. The guilty analyst resigned under pressure and, in exile, became the scapegoat for several influential analysts and candidates with similar sexual-ethical violations who remained within the fold. The process of scapegoating itself increased the potential and fear of further scapegoating. No one felt safe; everyone was under suspicion, yet no one within the institute wanted to open Pandora's box to further scrutiny, fearing for the reputations of men and women they loved and respected and fearing irreparable damage to the organization which continued to be important to them and their community.

Faced with recurrent waves of crisis, some of the candidates and analysts suggested outside consultation as a way to stop the vicious cycle of denial and accusation as well as explore organization-wide dynamics that seemed to be leading to more violations. Most members, especially those who had acted improperly and those who knew of such actions, were afraid to engage in what became labeled a witch hunt. They felt strongly that the organization should be able to take care of its own. Their leadership moved the institute to the writing of a new code of ethics, which in its development allowed some valuable discussion of the issues in the safety of abstraction. The code was used by other institutes wrestling with similar ethical problems. Its usefulness to others helped members recover somewhat from their badly injured esteem.

The immediate crisis seemed to be over. In the following few years, several analysts chose to drop out rather than deal with possible exposure; others left or became disinterested in the organization as the process of denial continued. Discussion of the underlying collective issues was held to a minimum. But while scapegoating and isolating dynamics remained ascendant, a counterforce also gained momentum. Outside consultation was obtained, not for epidemic ethical violations, but for financial problems. This led to a reorganization of the administration of the institute and its power structure, as well as a rethinking about tasks and goals. In addition, many small groups sprang up to deal with the unspoken anxieties of the membership and the deficiencies of its program in safe and structured ways. For example, there was exploration of clinical and style differences among various analysts, including discussions of the limits of intimacy and "dual" relationships in therapy. Colleague-centered supervision was established in the guise of studying the way the analytic process was being taught. A self-study group concerned with collective processes in the institute and an in-house journal were inaugurated, along with a "diversity" committee designed to make the institute more reflective of the larger community. All these changes seemed to move the institute toward taking more responsibility for its individual difficulties through education and openness rather than protectionism and denial. Thus the institute exhibited some aspects of a strong island mentality, and it was difficult for it or any of its parts, including the candidates, to receive outside help in an area in which it felt it already had sufficient expertise—psychological development. As long as its organizational identity relied on such a strong internal boundary, change remained an internal affair.

In my experience, these examples are typical of the way most groups function today. Groups in which the scapegoating or isolating consciousness does not play a central role are rare indeed. As Jung would have been the first to say, the commitment to individual development has just begun. Yet it seems that it is the creative marriage between individual and collective development that holds the key to our future as a species and as a planet. Depth psychology, with its previous emphasis on the individual expanded to include the collective, can help explore the mysteries of our sentient species, perhaps developing new post-scapegoating forms. They are not forms that any of us know much about, but which all of us must be bound and determined to discover if we value our species development and our future survival.

What hope can we find for such a profound change in the collective behavior and attitudes of our species as we approach the end of the twentieth century? Here we can turn to the world of archetypes, what Jung calls the "primordial" image.

> I call the image primordial when it possesses an *archaic* (q.v.) character. I speak of its archaic character when the image is in striking accord with familiar mythological motifs. It then expresses material primarily derived from the *collective unconscious* (q.v.) and indicates at the same time that the factors

influencing the conscious situation of the moment are collective rather than personal. . . .

The primordial image, elsewhere also termed *archetype*, is always collective, i.e., it is at least common to entire peoples or epochs. (1921, par. 746–747)

Can the underlying archetype of a society or a whole culture change? Jung proposed that one or another archetype could become dominant in a society and affect its cultural myths and social structures (ibid.). The great nineteenth-century historian Jacob Burkhardt demonstrated this principle brilliantly in his classic study of Renaissance Italy by defining a basic change in societal consciousness as the key to understanding the evolution between the medieval and Renaissance periods of Western history. He showed how medieval Christianity's belief in rebirth into an afterlife changed to the Renaissance *zeitgeist* of a rebirth which took place not after death but within individuals and their culture, through their bodies, work, art, and ideas.

Such a transformation, which changes the fundamental relationship between god and human and between human and human and affects everything from bedtime stories to family and government structures, falls into the category of an archetypal shift. It is this kind of massive shift in archetypal conscious that several modern scholars, notably Robert Lifton (1964) and Jonathan Schell (1982), have suggested is happening now as the potential consequences of nuclear power and the fragility of the ecological fabric of our planet penetrates world consciousness.

In the nuclear era, the archetype of Death-and-Rebirth is being replaced by what I term Death-without-Rebirth, what Raymond Hillis has called the "image of annihilation" (1985, p. 51). Apocalyptic visions of world destruction have been part of our collective mythology all along, and war, plagues, floods, earthquakes, and other catastrophes lend substance to these images. Yet rebirth has been a critical element in the archetype; Death-and-Rebirth has been a central image for the human species. Jung (1952) spent many volumes tracing the archetype of rebirth through patients, students, cultures, and historical change. We seem to have a profound *biosocial intuition* that growth and change follows loss and stagnation.

The new archetype, spawned by the nuclear and environmental

reality and increasingly informing our collective, is Death-with-out-Rebirth. This is not only about whether or not a nuclear war will destroy life forever or even about the psychological mecha-nism of denial implicit in the manufacture of each new nuclear warhead or toxic chemical. The archetype is a new underlying premise, a new pattern of image/thought/feeling which is unconscious and pervasive, and it is antithetical to our previous worldview. It is, however, an archetype that has been gradually emerging from the collective unconscious for many centuries. Its increasing importance has been implicit in the deconstruction and mythologizing of heaven and hell in traditional religions and in the ascending scientific and humanistic points of view, while the counterweights of renewed fundamentalism and new-age spirituality attest to the continuing power of the archetype of rebirth in the human collective.

The two archetypes are often confused in an effort not to confront their conflicting theme. Examples include apocalyptic denial, as in religious prophesies of a new and better order emerging out of a nuclear "cleansing," or a kind of evolutionary "realism," the promise to ourselves that some life will go on even if the human species doesn't. Such structures of denial, like most of our military and environmental strategies during the past forty years, are best understood as reactions to two archetypes in colli-sion. They all contain a great deal of creativity and suppression, and even some insanity. Reality in the nuclear era is simultane-ously as it has been and profoundly different from before; and we need to explore this reality with psychological theories capable of dealing meaningfully with such profound changes.

In particular, we know little about the effect of a shift in archetypes on political systems for which war, made tenable through the aegis of the Death-and-Rebirth archetype, has always been the final arbiter of change. Unfortunately, neither political analysts nor politicians themselves are used to dealing with the unconscious assumptions behind their behavior.

In the essay "The Undiscovered Self," Jung's profound worry about the nuclear threat spurred him to attempt a rare statement linking individual and group consciousness.

> But fear of the evil which one does not see in one's own
> bosom, always in somebody else's, checks reason every time,

although everyone knows that the use of this weapon means the certain end of our present human world. . . . If only a world-wide consciousness could arise that all division and all fission are due to the splitting of opposites in the psyche, then we should know where to begin. But if even the smallest and most personal stirrings of the individual psyche—so insignificant in themselves—remain as unconscious and unrecognized as they have hitherto, they will go on accumulating and produce mass groupings and mass movements which cannot be subjected to reasonable control or manipulated to a good end. (1957, par. 574).

Jung's own conundrum here as elsewhere is that the problem of effecting such an enlightened "world-wide consciousness" is also the problem of effecting some positive change in world-wide group development and therefore in the political structures of the mass man in which, as we know, Jung had no expressed hope. His own enduring psyche split between individual and group, and the inevitable inflation of one at the expense of the other left him unable to conceive of individuation occurring in any human matrix other than the individual human being, in whom, as Jung says at the end of his essay, "even God seeks his goal" (ibid., par. 588).

Mary Renault's book *The King Must Die* (1958) follows the journey of Theseus as he reenacts the classic myth of death and rebirth—the sacrifice of the young king to the requirements of society for new forms to develop. It is a familiar myth—a sad story with a hopeful ending. One of the burdens our society faces today is the loss of this old and bittersweet story. Having replaced the King with democracy—a group project—we now find ourselves writing a new story entitled *The Group Must Die*. Species progress and even survival now depend on collective as well as individual development. As this concept becomes more acceptable, it will provide its own evolutionary push toward greater collective consciousness, a process already underway.[7]

The greatest challenge to our survival may well be the huge inertia in our political systems and particularly its extroverted politicians. Such action-oriented individuals, when faced with difficult problems, are prone to redesign and restructure, and if that fails, destroy and rebuild (as our military history amply

91

documents). But the new archetype gives greater impetus to more introverted and process-centered strategies of education and training. The development of methods for depth exploration of group and organizational process can be seen as an outgrowth of this need. It is not surprising, given the tension between the two worldviews, that leadership is ambivalent about such modes of learning. For example, at one group relations conference with the task of studying unconscious behavior in groups, which included a number of high-ranking politicians, several national congressmen, and major-city police chiefs, my staff and I were told that the day-to-day problems they face in the political arena and the process those problems evoked were simply qualitatively different than the problems and processes they experienced in other groups, particularly groups with a "learning task." In fact, their behavior during the conference itself had sought (with some success) to shift the study task to a more familiar, safety-factored pragmatic mode where they could use their tried and true "art of the possible" approach.

Recent diplomatic and military intervention is faced with similar tensions, as Americans discovered in ambivalent encounters with Iraq, Somalia, the Balkan states, and Haiti. Diplomats and generals carry this conflict for all of us as we factor in images of total annihilation with conventional truths about the use of massive physical force to impose one collective's will on another. What is increasingly clear and so hard to accept, is that taken alone the "art of the possible" is an anachronism in the nuclear era. In that mode, we are still denying the underlying difference between prenuclear political problems and the nuclear dilemma, between the two competing archetypes of Death-and-Rebirth and Death-without-Rebirth. What is political process in this new mode? I don't think we know yet, and I do not believe we have really completely engaged the issue. We need a model, probably many models, which include structure and process, pragmatics and myth, conscious and unconscious realities, to study how to understand, how to gauge the effects; we need these models to deal with and dream in the new reality.

The possibility of death without rebirth is becoming our myth; it will remain our myth for the foreseeable future. It is not necessarily a story of a sacrifice for a new order. It may find its source in the ultimate act of species death, or it may be far more positive, a new process for living together. To survive, the myths we embrace will surely not rest on the old ways of scapegoating and isolation. The scapegoats might steal a nuclear warhead; the isolated might pollute the ocean and destroy the rain forests. Myths of interdependence, such as Arthur's Round Table and the shaman's reciprocity, carry more hope in a world on which boundaries of air, water, earth, and fire are increasingly more relevant than maps of nations or even the classification of species. We can muscle solutions with our new technologies and organizational strategies, or we can be open to guidance from new myths, still nascent in our collective—myths which hold for the web as well as the spider, and which name humankind as just one of many life forms caught in its grand design. It remains to be seen whether we can find the answer in our own collective spirit.

6

Depth Consultation in Organizations: Awakening Collective Consciousness

FROM THE PERSPECTIVE OF THE INITIATED SHAMANIC HEALER, the journey into the "other world" is rarely self-authorized and never without intent. Rather, the shaman seeks that world in order to serve this one. The quest is for a vision at the behest of the collective for a particular purpose. Most of the time the intent of the journey is to heal—heal the individual, heal the community. The wisdom of the shaman is as much in accomplishing this work without losing sight of his or her authorization and task as in the skill and artistry of dealing with the "other world."

In the largest sense of his role, the shaman affirms the presence of a world beyond the community's ordinary reality. He adds meaning to its members' lives and makes the world beyond a locus of creativity and healing. In this chapter, following this perspective, I want to consider how we can use our modern knowledge of the unconscious to serve groups and communities by consulting to their "other world"—the world of group archetypes which underlie, give meaning, and have potential for creativity and healing.

For the past twenty years, I have had the good fortune to be a Jungian analyst working primarily with individuals and also an organizational consultant trained in the tradition of Tavistock group relations, working with groups and communities. Early on, the above description of group consultation, what I call depth consultation, was a better description of my work with individuals in Jungian analysis than consultation to groups. Organizational work was pragmatic and functional; whereas Tavistock work, while committed to exploring the unconscious of groups, defined that unconscious more narrowly than Jung's collective psychology allowed. Over the years, the two perspectives and the two roles have grown together. I find that the way I fill the role of analyst and consultant is powerfully informed and energized by the other. I find that the systems of individual and collective have grown together as well, that each can be seen and felt as a representation of the other, different lenses through which a more basic organizing consciousness is perceived.

One of the more important organizing concepts in either system is individuation.[8] Jung assigns this process exclusively to the individual but in theory it can be applied to any system, including groups and collectives that seek a unique wholeness. Jung himself spent the largest part of his later writings devoted to amplifying, through the metaphors of alchemy and other transformational spiritual disciplines, the many paths through which the struggle for wholeness may be lived out by the individual. One of the hallmarks of these descriptions, as I discussed in chapter 1, is the polarity between the individual-in-process and the static collective from which the individual differentiates: the individual is the "diamond" to be liberated from the collective "rough." Jung is more pessimistic about transforming groups, except through a developed individual's efforts in groups. Although he rarely speaks directly to the concept of service to the collective, how this might be done, for example, in an analogous way to the way the analyst serves the individual, he does warn that individuation is an isolating path. In one early statement, he speaks of the ongoing relationship between individual and collective in a particularly insightful way.

> Individuation cuts one off from personal conformity and hence from collectivity. That is the guilt which the individuant leaves behind him for the world, that is the guilt he must endeavor to redeem. He must offer a ransom in place of

himself, that is, he must bring forth values which are an equivalent substitute for his absence in the collective personal sphere. Without this production of values, final individuation is immoral and—more than that—suicidal. The man who cannot create values should sacrifice himself consciously to the spirit of collective conformity. . . . Not only has society a right, it also has a duty to condemn the individuant if he fails to create equivalent values, for he is a deserter. (1916, par. 1095–96)

Jung's pessimism about transforming collective process except through transforming individual process is also mirrored in many Jungian analysts' cynical view of the value of direct service to the collective. An extreme but not atypical viewpoint is illustrated by the answer to a question I once posed to a revered teacher: "How does individuation serve the collective?" Her apocryphal answer was: "If I walk alone on the beach intent on my own individuation, then and only then do I truly serve others. Service to others begins and ends in my own development." Certainly the quality of service is dependent on self-knowledge. Yet the answer to my question or even to the question, "Does individuation always serve the collective?" may not be as straightforward as this teacher would want.

Jung himself suggests that working out one's individual destiny for oneself is not always valuable to the collective: one may be a "deserter," much as a parent may desert the family, or a leader may desert the group, all in the name of a quest for individuation. There must be equivalent value, says Jung, or the damage done to a family or a community in the name of individuation can transform a sacred quest into a "suicidal" venture. Moreover, what may feel like a hero's "individuation" journey may also be a group "setup" of an innocent who carries the sins of others. Sometimes the individual walking on the beach is on a journey that will benefit self and others too, and sometimes he or she will be unwittingly caught in the archetype of the scapegoat for the collective; those heroic solitary walks may at times be more in the service of keeping falsehood alive in others than truth alive in oneself.

At the heart of such dilemmas is the tendency to separate the individual from the collective and individual development

97

from collective development. Individuation in the adult may begin in separation from the collective, much as individuation in the young child may begin in separation from the parent(s). But separation from the collective is not the aim of individuation; rather, it is one of the paths some people use to learn more about themselves away from the influences of others. In group relations theory, there is a concept known as "group in the mind" which expresses the ever-present group consciousness of individuals even and especially when they are most isolated and functioning most separately from others. We are always collective entities as much as individual entities.

Individuation of the individual cannot proceed without a concomitant developmental process in the collective, and here timing may be a critical dimension for the fate of the development of both. In some cultures, rites of initiation use the consciousness-altering property of isolation to intensify a feeling of disconnection from the collective and accentuate the awareness of one's own uniqueness and unique mission (Henderson 1967). Individuals subjected to such ordeals often hallucinate or have visions (depending on the collective's definition of the experience), and these extraordinary experiences often provide a new frame of identity for the individuals and a new role in the collective. But the collective—be it family, community, work, or spiritual environment—must be developmentally ready to honor these visions, or else the new role of the visionary in the collective may be as patient in a mental hospital. No matter how powerfully charged these metaphorical walks on the beach are for the individual, their transformative potential will always depend on the state of the collective.

In a very real sense, then, individual and collective development are inextricably intertwined. We know this well from studying the wounded children of undeveloped families and finding it necessary to work with families as part of the task of healing these wounds. Nor is individuation ever an individual process for long; developing individuals will soon enough be measured by self and group in the way they serve, and serve in, the community. From an ethical point of view, individuation defined outside of its collective context is a travesty, because it separates individual development from the suffering of others. From a psychological point of view, individuation separate from the collective is flawed, because it leaves the shadow out of the process. The personal shadow is projected onto the collective scapegoat, and then one turns one's back on that scapegoat and calls it simply a product of a "lower level of consciousness" or "mass mind." But the "mass mind" is us, the product of our collective projections, what we can't handle in ourselves. Individuation requires acceptance of our responsibility for the suffering and scapegoating in the collective and a commitment to help, not just our selves and our kin, but our collective as well. It is no accident that men and women who have achieved universal recognition for spiritual development—Christ, Gandhi, Mother Teresa, Martin Luther King Jr.—have devoted themselves to helping the poor, the homeless, the diseased, the suffering—*our* victims.

There are many academic disciplines that deal directly with the psychology of the collective and the pragmatics of how to help it develop—sociology and political science, to name the two most prominent. And beyond the university, methods abound which purport to help understand and improve groups and their collective functioning—methods subsumed under the rubric of organizational development. "Community building," "leadership training," "team building," and "negotiation strategies" are some of the buzz words for these approaches. With a few important exceptions, these disciplines, both academic and pragmatic, do not aim to connect their work to the unconscious process of the collective; yet there are few who doubt that many organizations and all governments need help for their irrational processes. We need only to consider how much the antagonistic polarity between the two superpowers of the Cold War was a psychological projection rather than a pragmatic reality to appreciate how many resources are being spent on the myths of group process.

The resistance to exploring even such obvious group dynamics is extremely powerful. Neither nations and organizations nor smaller groups necessarily want to look deeply into their origins, their myths, and their complexes—the ways the collective unconscious manifests in their structures and processes. Who knows what would be found and how the status quo would be changed by what is found? Nor do consultants, even if they believe that the source of conflict and healing lies in that realm, necessarily look in that direction. Those who hire

99

such consultants almost always feel that they have the most to lose. Neither a culture of collective exploration nor a consulting methodology to assist such an exploration has yet developed parallel to the ethos that fuels individual exploration and depth therapies. To achieve this, we need an unaccusing perspective which assumes that the collective unconscious operates in and through groups and organizations as well as in and through individuals, that the two are connected.

How might such a perspective operate through the consultation process? When I consult with these principles in mind, I start off with the same assumption that informs my exploration of an individual seeking help in analysis: I assume that the organization has integrity beyond its individual members, much as the individual has integrity beyond the ego's attitudes or the dominant complex. I also assume that every organization is capable of developing in order to manifest its deepest identity, what could be called its organizational self, much as the individual is guided by the capacity to realize his or her self.

The organizational self, like the individual self, is what a given organization seeks to become—the unfolding of its potential, its inexorable movement toward integration and wholeness. Just as the infant self develops in relation to its developmental needs, the early enfolding of the organizational self is filtered through the task system which defines its developmental identity. Eric Erickson (1972) wisely pointed out that identity formation is always as much a function of who one is not as who one is. An organization develops, much like a child, by fashioning a provisional identity which excludes and represses those parts which are troublesome and dystonic. Early in most organizations' lives, there is the need for cohesion which denies the complexity and confusion inherent in origin and task. Projection and repression are used in the service of furthering this cohesion; the price is exclusion of dissident elements and a loss of wholeness until reintegration is possible.

In the individual, these excluded elements coalesce in what Jung called the shadow—that part of us that is deeply unacceptable to the ego. Confronting and reintegrating the shadow is, from the point of view of Jungian analysis, the sine qua non of individuation. So, too, with organizations, whose excluded parts hold the creative and change-producing elements without which stagnation is all but inevitable. Like the adult who must reclaim and acknowledge these discarded and repressed parts in order to feel whole and real, the mature organization must struggle to include what has been left out, pushed out, denied and ignored in order to function at the highest level. Thus, from the point of view of collective as well as individual development, the shadow—individual and collective—must be acknowledged and reclaimed for the self to operate fully and transformatively.

In depth consultation, then, as in analysis, I assume that development must include the reintegration of a scapegoated part of the organization, the organization's shadow. (This approach differs from the more usual kinds of organizational consultation, which deal with what is working and what will make it work better.) Because my concern is always with the individuation of the organization, my initial consulting task is to define these scapegoated elements, explore the scapegoating process, and give meaning to both as they manifest in the functions and goals of the organization. The implicit consulting contract I use includes client acceptance of this perspective, a willingness to join with me in this exploration—no matter where it leads.

The actual act of consulting gives one a chance to explore such processes in greater detail, much as therapy or analysis provides that opportunity with an individual. My own experience is that even when I am welcomed into a group or organization, even when an adequate consulting alliance seems to be developing, when methods for providing access to the group consciousness are embraced, the tendency to blame or see solutions within individuals, rather than center on the collective process itself, remains very strong and will undermine most other processes unless it is exposed. From the group's point of view, then, it is easy to see why the consultant poses such a threat and can be so easily waylaid in his or her task: just as the individual sees the impersonal group as a danger to his or her development, so the group, taken as a unit, sees the unaffiliated and "unsocialized" individual—in this case, the consultant—as a danger to its status quo, its current definition of itself. That is, the group will defend its integrity, its wholeness, against all attempts at redefinition. The consultant to the group, like the analyst in the dyad, is always challenging the way things are, always pushing the boundaries of definitions and assumptions.

Even though the group members know that this is the task the consultant, whom they have hired, will perform, the group will consciously and unconsciously deal with this threat by walling off the consultant into a role in which he or she is symbolically destroyed, that is, rendered unable to work. This is akin to the way patients sometimes develop a stereotypic transference toward the analyst—"You are just like my mother" (or "my father")—as a way to change a mysterious and potentially unstabilizing relationship into one which, if painful or stultifying, is still known and therefore secure. As we know from analysis, the seeds of real change are encoded in the understanding and transformation of the transference. Unlocking that code requires interpretation of the transference in an atmosphere of safety. In the individual analytic situation, there is the potential for a gradual formulation of the transference and a honing of the accuracy of interpretation through conscious and unconscious feedback in the dyad. But while the same decoding process is necessary in the transference to the group consultant, it is far more difficult to develop a safe and trusting container for the necessary interpretation. In group work, there is often less time to develop interpretations in a timely framework and there is always a potential scapegoat for an undeveloped, uncommitted group to blame. Failing all else, the consultant is ready-made for that scapegoat role—perfectly cast, as it were, as the cause rather than the cure for a group's problems. As uncomfortable as this may be for the consultant, interpreting to the group this blatantly self-defeating dynamic may be the beginning of the deeper aspect of collective work.

Thus the group consultation contract is, in fact, much like the contract between individual patient and analyst, an agreement to explore shadow and other unconscious elements to enhance meaning and self-definition. For example, organizations, like both individuals and nations, are often unconsciously driven by their myth of origin. During my work with a client organization, I might explore its particular myth of origin, its birth or rebirth history, parental images, utopian visions, and so on in order to bring the meaning of these elements into the organization's consciousness, much as an analyst might explore origin and other unconscious motifs with the analysand for the same reason. My experience of doing this kind of work as either depth consultant or analyst is remarkably alike in some basic ways. Of course, there are technical differences, especially in pace and timing; organizational consulting tends to be less leisurely than analysis and may require more aggressive interpretation. But the similarities outweigh differences.

In individual work, the analyst elicits history, dreams, fantasy, relationship, and transference material, to help the analysand explore his or her unconscious world of complexes and processes; the organizational consultant elicits similar material from individuals, subgroups, and intergroups within the organization in order to develop a map of the client group's unconscious world. Individual analytic work proceeds on an inner psychic stage across which the figures of the unconscious play out the hoped-for psychic transformation; the analyst stands, one foot in that stage and one foot in the wings, anchoring the developmental process. In depth consultation, the consultant takes up the same boundary-straddling and anchoring position, except that the players are real members of the organization and the consulting work is helping to sort through these patterns until the central myths are clarified and their meaning for the organization better understood.

From the analyst's and consultant's point of view, working with individual or organization is like working with siblings who share the same parent. The collective pattern of behavior in the organization, the dream of an individual, the outward play of an organizational myth, the inward play of an individual myth—all have common roots in the collective unconscious. Individual analysts or organizational consultants who are committed to depth exploration locate themselves at the border of the imaginal space of either system—listening, exploring, and interpreting the stuff of the unconscious, be it dream, fantasy, ritual patterns, myth, interpersonal drama, interorganizational rivalry—all elements of the deepening search for meaning and transformation.

With groups, even more than with individuals, the consultant has to decide how much he or she will intervene in the process as it unfolds, how much to provide additional media and experimental material to open the door yet a little wider to that "other world." I speak here of ecstatic group methods such as drumming, chanting, and meditating, which build group consciousness by emphasizing the commonness beyond individuality and the ancient species crèche which unites us all.

And always, in both systems, there is a missing element, an excluded part, the personal shadow, the collective scapegoat, standing in the way of the search and containing its central meaning. In organizational life, the scapegoat holds the hidden corruption, the unspeakable scandals, the dark side, much as the shadow constellates these elements in the individual. *The scapegoat and the scapegoating process often hold the unconscious problem of the organization, that which must sooner or later be confronted and reintegrated if change is to occur.*

All organizations work hard, consciously and unconsciously, to protect both the scapegoating process and their chosen scapegoats. This is in the nature of the archetype of the scapegoat, "the one who has been made to take the blame for others or to suffer in their place." An organization will not easily give up a well-worn pattern of projecting its most unacceptable parts onto an available victim. Part of the art of consultation is how to ferret out the manifestation of this scapegoat archetype without losing one's client. Consultants and whistle blowers know too well the great danger of meddling with an entrenched scapegoating system. In the Bible story of the scapegoat, the man who takes the scapegoat into the wilderness is in great danger. In practice, the man who speaks the truth about the scapegoat often shares its fate.

In my experience, the most common reason for a dynamic of scapegoating to develop in an organization is fear of confronting real and imagined difference in the collective (Colman 1989). If the challenge of diversity becomes great enough to threaten the perceived cohesion, unity, and ultimately the survival of the group, the group will defend itself by invoking the scapegoating process. Or, put another way, groups, like individuals, are always in pursuit of wholeness and, like individuals who reject shadow elements of themselves by projecting them out onto the environment, groups will create victims rather than face dealing with diversity and difference.

Typically, consultation requests usually carry within them this scapegoat issue, almost always defined from the victimizer's point of view. Thus, there is a defined "problem," "without whom" all would be well (or at least better). On one occasion, I was asked by the literature department of a large midwestern university to consult around a "difficult" assistant professor who was being denied tenure despite obvious academic excellence. The denial related to a particular "impropriety" in his behavior, an alleged slanderous remark toward one of his fellow tenure seekers. The department was afraid that he might protest the department's action. On another occasion, I was asked to consult to the upper management of a government agency whose *esprit de corps* was being "undermined" by the agency's clients, "misguided" citizens who "misapprehended" the agency's policies and now were threatening to sue the agency. On a third occasion, I was asked to consult to a small business because one of the partners, who had a particularly important technical skill, was acting in a way that was jeopardizing the whole operation and refusing to change his behavior. In all these examples, the organization as a whole was faced with a challenge from an important constituent part— junior faculty, consumer citizens, and a powerful partner. In each case, the leadership perceived threat to its wholeness and its authority. Consultation had been requested because the scapegoating hadn't worked: the scapegoating process, developed to rid the organization of its dissidents, had aborted and the bloody remains were still in evidence and threatening the organization with infection. From the excluding subsystem's point of view, the dissident part (individual, group, department, or even nation) is seen as a pathological entity, the isolated problem, trial without argument, the verdict already in. The tenure candidate was a loser but could make trouble; the consumers were misguided but could undermine policy and funding; the partner was acting inappropriately but could break up the company. All that was required was a consultant who, as an outside authority, would sanction the exclusion and recommend what was needed—reeducation, treatment, or even annihilation—the final solution. The professor needed therapy for his aggression; the citizens were misguided and needed further education; the partner was pigheaded and must learn to give in to the needs of others or get out.

In practice, the individual is rarely an innocent in the organizational process. Groups choose their victims well, and most victims have a way of volunteering for the job. The consultant brought into a scapegoating situation is inevitably asked to accept the organization's point of view and divert attention from the system's problem to the "disturbed" individual. It is quite a temptation, since the organization, not the scapegoat, is paying the consultant's bill. But whatever the balance between individual and organization, the individual who has been selected for victimhood is rarely able to hold his or her own. The power of the organization or majority culture to create victims for its own psychological purpose is the power of the many over the few. Only very courageous or foolhardy individuals or subgroups can stand up to a powerful victim-creating process. To help an organization, the consultant must refocus attention on how the need for a scapegoat and the choice of victim is a diversion from the deeper collective issues.

The tactical problem for the consultant is how to gain sufficient trust within the organization to redefine the scapegoating process as a part of the organization's troubled process rather than its cause. The consultant faces a problem similar to that of the analyst with a patient who defines his or her symptom—anxiety, nightmares, a compulsive affair—as the problem without which there would be no problem. In individuals, where symptoms are part of a larger problem, shadow elements are breaking through the ego's defensive edifice, an attenuated structure based on an incomplete view of itself. Often it is easier to embrace mendacity and medication than to consider the symptom as pointing to a larger problem. The analytic, explorative mode depends on a willingness to search for meaning in the excluding and isolating patterns. Then the symptoms are useful; they forcefully pose the problem of false integrity and point to what has been defensively excluded and what now must be redeemed.

Depth consultation requires the same mutual willingness to search for meaning in the excluding scapegoating pattern. For the organization, the presence of a noncompliant member is like anxiety to the individual, and the dynamic of scapegoating is a particularly efficient "medication," a "solution"; when it works, the unwanted parts can be permanently expunged and, like the biblical scapegoat, exiled to the wilderness, never to return. That is the hope at least, but as the Israelites found in their sojourn in the wilderness, the excluding ritual must be repeated to have even minimal cathartic effect on the collective. And, as Saul found when he tried to exclude a dissident David from his ranks, scapegoats have a way of turning up with large armies (or a bevy of lawyers) in pursuit of their definitions of justice.

I want now to turn to two consultations in which the dynamics of exclusion and scapegoating were prominent.

Consultation 1

I consulted to a top management group—sixteen men and women—of a government agency in California concerned with conservation. The agency was embattled by a well-organized group of citizens who were opposed to the way government leadership carried out its mandate and made policy. I was asked by the agency director to help develop more-successful approaches to the problem than the management group had thus far been able to devise.

I met with the entire group for a weekend retreat. I soon discovered that the director was convinced of the "goodness" of the way he and his management were performing. He said esprit was high and performance had improved in response to the current stress. He felt policy was well thought out and relevant to task. He was sure the agency was capable of changing its ideas and process if needed; that was not a problem—witness the successful incorporation of affirmative action hiring policies amply demonstrated by the women and minority present in the room. "This group," the director proudly told me, with affirming nods from the people in the room, "is like a good American family. We care about our own, and we take care of our own. And we have tried-and-true family ways of changing things when they need changing."

Obviously, a great deal was being left out. I have learned over the course of many consulting efforts that whenever family metaphors are used to describe organizations, it is likely that the exclusion dynamic is particularly insidious. Hallowed family platitudes often hide a multitude of family sins, including incest, sexism, and "black sheep" victimizations, to mention a few. Organizations are not families, and those that claim to be are usually profoundly afraid of their secrets and their differences. I listened sympathetically for a long time, considering how to intervene and discarding every intervention that came to mind. My silence was irritating to the group. They were not paying me a

107

good fee to be a noncontributor. They continued to speak about their cohesion and shared values, their ability to integrate one and all into their "family." When and whether I would join was the unspoken question of the group.

When the question of my inclusion was finally made overt by one of the leaders, I made my move. "If everything is so good," I chided gently, "then who are the public that seem to disagree with your policies? Why don't they feel part of your family? Who might they represent here? Is anybody feeling left out of the family here and now in this room, the way those citizens feel left out of your decision-making process and your decisions?"

At first, there was polite but hostile silence to my remark. This was followed by even more fervent demonstrations of harmony and familyhood. But as I persisted in asking the same series of questions in a variety of ways, the group turned on me with more open anger. Apparently, they had gotten the wrong consultant. I obviously didn't understand either, anymore than the citizen's group and other detractors understood. Perhaps only family members could get it right. "Well, if that's true," I said, "then where does that leave those of us who aren't family—like the group of citizens, who aren't family, perhaps don't want to be family, but still want to get some of their needs met. Doesn't any one here identify with them rather than this family?"

No one did, which led to more rancor with me, diluted only by the congenial surroundings and good food. My questions and their patience were wearing thin. Some kind of breakthrough had to occur soon or I would be out of a job and the agency would be even more isolated than before. Searching for a chink in the armor, I asked the women present if they really felt part of the family (which seemed to me to be increasingly defined as an "old boy" network). "Yes indeed," one exclaimed, "we are just that and proud of it." There was a chorus of assent from most of the women, who went on to explain that those women who had made it in the agency were indeed daughters and wives of men who worked or had worked in the agency! "It is a big, happy family," they chided back. Didn't I see that now?

When I wondered about what such a kinship hiring pattern meant in a government agency—was only "family" to be trusted?—the group again defended itself. It obviously made sense to hire people who knew the job and were "blood-loyal," as

108

one put it. But the silence that followed this rejoinder was less smug than before. Something was wrong; everyone could feel it. There was a piece missing and attempts to get on with other business fell flat.

"Is everybody here really a part of this wonderful family?" I asked, more cynically than I wished. "Am I the only one who has another family to go home to at night?" I looked significantly at each person in turn and then shut up. This was the moment of truth, the one on which the consultation would probably turn.

To my great relief, a black woman stood up and faced the group. "Hell no," she exclaimed, "I'm not a part of this family. I've got my own family. I'm working here because the money is good. I'm also here to do what I can to stop the rest of you from stealing the public land for yourselves and your fat white 'families.' And there's no way you're going to get rid of me for saying this. You need me and you know it. And this consultant is my witness, even if he is a honkie."

After a stunned silence, a young white man with longish hair stood up. "This isn't my family either. No way. I want to change things, bring in some new-age values. The citizen's group is right about some things. It's going to change around here whether you guys like it or not."

Gradually others in the group followed their lead in speaking up, some still identifying with the family, others opposing it in one way or another. There was a lot of mourning the loss of the "good old days," which, as so often is the case, turned out to be less halcyon than legend claimed.

The rest of the weekend was a long amplification of the theme of the need to learn how to let in difference, change, new people, and new ways. While the exclusionary dynamic continued to emerge at times of greatest disagreement, I could now consult to it and find some joining voices. While I had no illusions that the organization as whole would drastically change its view toward outside criticism, a small inroad had been made, including some understanding of the problem, and more consultation was likely. The seed for future change had definitely been planted.

My interventions were based on the hypothesis that the excluded or scapegoated elements of an organizational system carry its development potential, much as the shadow carries that potential in the individual. This agency's reaction to criticism from the citizen's group was to exclude their views and create an even more islandlike mentality called "family." Certainly this response was counterproductive to their task. It seemed likely to me that the outside group had struck important unidentified views and feelings within the agency itself, whose "family romance" effectively excluded criticism and difference in its members, let alone in those it served—the public. The negotiations with the citizen's group could not be effective until this undercover dynamic inside the agency was brought to light. In the intense atmosphere of a weekend group retreat, exploring what different views from the citizen's group might symbolize and mirror in the management group was potentially explosive. Once the challenge to the family fantasy was out in the open, once the "black sheep" were brought to light, the agency leadership would have a better chance to develop on more realistic grounds and find a new myth that better fit its present and future.

Consultation 2

I was asked to consult to a large organization which provided many highly valued services in health, education, and business within its target community, a multinational immigrant population. The organization was composed of first-generation immigrants and first-generation U.S. citizens, and it was typical of similar organizations which serve immigrants from geographical areas such as the Pacific Rim, Central America, or the Middle East, in which internecine struggle is a fact of life. Many of the homeland countries have been at war or in serious conflict with one another. Many people have died in these wars, and many of the staff and clients were refugees from war. In effect, this background insured that staff subgroups felt like enemies; in some cases, only their transplanted geography prevented them from being in a live war. And yet, within the United States, as has happened to so many immigrant groups before them, these virtual enemies were lumped together into a single organization and client system. In particular, funding was dependent on a racist assumption that lumped people together on the basis of skin color or facial characteristics. They were treated by government as if they were homogeneous, a single ethnic unity who could identify with and serve one another, when in fact their diversity was extreme and saturated in intergroup violence. Here, the scapegoating dynamic was already present in the relationship with the culture at large. One could predict that the leadership of such an organization would have an impossible and intolerable task, that any functional system which represented integration in the face of such violent opposition would come under attack.

The stated problem for which consultation was requested was recurrent instability in the organization's leadership. Two previous directors, both highly qualified and acceptable to staff at their hiring, had been fired or had resigned in the past two years. The current director, L., was equally well qualified, but he was now also being pressured to leave after only six months on the job.

When I first met with L. to consider our consultation contract, he suggested intensive work with the staff as a group. In view of the inflammatory nature of the problem, I proposed instead a careful diagnostic program through a series of meetings with key personnel, to be followed by meetings with various subgroups of staff before dealing with the staff as a whole. But the next day, there was another major leadership crisis, and the entire staff demanded a meeting with the director in the presence of the consultant. When L. told me about this request, he confirmed that he was being asked to resign. It was not the ideal way to begin a consulting job.

The meeting began with a dissection of L.'s personal and leadership characteristics, emphasizing his authoritarianism and his incompetence. Some of the group began to infer that he was also clinically paranoid and thereby unfit to lead. These accusations found few "hooks" in the face of L.'s competent and judicious behavior during his short tenure as leader. L. pointed out that similar defamations had also been leveled at the previous directors. This defense was met with redoubled attacks; at one point, the group asked me, now labeled as a psychiatrist rather than organizational consultant, to "certify" L. as insane. When I demurred, suggesting that such a pronouncement was beyond

111

my role, the opposition leadership in the group seemed to give up all rational pretense. One of the informal leaders of the staff group put it bluntly: "Even if L. is mentally fit," he said, "and even if L. is a decent leader, he still has to be sacrificed. There is just too much tension with him around. He must resign."

My authority to consult to this particular meeting was extremely limited. I was a stranger in the group and had had little opportunity to develop trust from either director or staff. Still, I needed to speak to the issue; I felt I would probably not get another chance. So I consulted directly to the scapegoating process by interpreting what seemed to me to be the most overt politic of the group—that the leader was being used as a convenient lightning rod to project anger more appropriately focused on the intergroup and international conflicts within the staff as well as on the racism implicit in their funding sources.

There was little discussion of my point; it was a premature interpretation born of impotence rather that ripeness. I knew that the intergroup rivalry was so acute that even focusing on the outside bureaucracy, a universal scapegoat in industrialized society, was unlikely to be heard. They were afraid of any agreement, because it would risk violating profound ethnic and national loyalties. The only acceptable common target was the leader himself, who symbolized their taboo interconnections. He was available as the unifying scapegoat because getting rid of him, as they had gotten rid of leaders before him, would perpetuate the chaos. They epitomized, in microcosm, the social structure of denial, the use of real and symbolic human sacrifice, and the victimization of the innocent to circumvent responsible confrontation with extremely difficult realities.

The process I was observing was indeed archetypal. L., as leader-scapegoat, had become an enormously useful vehicle for the collective shadow of this group, uniting the various warring subgroups in ritual murder. Guilt would come later, but for now the scapegoat archetype and the ancient dynamic of human sacrifice left no room for reason and rationality. The scapegoat holds the pain and suffering for the group—pain and suffering which the group can no longer handle within its own boundaries but must project and expel from its midst. The scapegoating process must be swift and merciless; the humanity of the victim must be denied. Anything less would elicit sympathy and support and the possibility of more explicit examination of the conflicts between member and member, subgroup and subgroup—which in this organization would move quickly into ancient and modern blood feuds. These issues were indeed explosive and would have to be approached with great care. The staff was not ready to do this, and so the leader-scapegoat had to go.

The entire staff seemed united in this process, except for one man, M., a business student interning with the organization. Like L., he was more identified with the organization as a whole than the internecine struggles of the subgroups. Soon after my comments, M. spoke out forcefully in the group. He said he agreed with what I had said; he, too, felt scapegoated in this organization whenever he openly identified with the organization as more than a collection of ethnic subgroups. After his speech, the staff turned on M. with a fury almost equal to its attack on L., but he countered by repeating his interpretation and suggested that the irrational fury of the attack was more evidence of what he was saying. Eventually, the group turned from him to the more satisfying massacre of L.

In chapter 1, I discussed Ursula K. Le Guin's walkaways and suggested that there was a kind of walkaway who rejects the system without leaving it. These "interpreters" locate themselves on the boundary of the scapegoating system, a dangerous stance. Students, because of their liminality and their youth, often have been able to speak from such a position of truth; many societies use students this way, although the tragedies of Kent State and Tiananmen Square suggest no absolute immunity. The business student intern, M., was an interpreter type by nature, and he was able to talk directly to the difficult issue confronting the group. He had less to lose than the paid employees and knew he could count on the support of his university and its teachers. Still, in the throes of an active scapegoating process, it takes great courage to speak out against the group norm and risk the danger of deadly contagion.

Neither my comments nor those of M., however, made a significant difference. The scapegoating forces were already too strong. When the meeting ended, L. was all but excommunicated. With the last shreds of his authority, he did authorize and pay for a consultation report, but he was fired a week after the meeting.

113

I heard nothing from the organization for five years, and then I received a phone call from M. He introduced himself as the new director, the third since L. had been fired. While going through the papers of his predecessor, M. had come upon my report gathering dust in a file cabinet. He was interested in my elaboration of the scapegoating phenomena and wanted to learn more about the model I was using and also what I might suggest to insure some longevity to his leadership. Could we talk in my office? This request began a five-year bimonthly consulting relationship which by all ordinary measures has been a great success. The organization is now known nationally as a model for working efficiently in a multiracial, multilingual setting. The greatest danger to M. is the parade of headhunters that pursue him.

What has changed? In our initial strategy session, M. said that the scapegoating system was still intact. He was sure it would destroy him if not held in check. My consultation report had given him an intellectual understanding of the powerful dynamic and also some hope for the future. We wondered aloud together about the growth and creativity possible if the organization did not divert so much of its energy toward the costly and painful biyearly crucifixion of its director and concentrated instead on the real tasks of development and service. But how to change that? Another direct interpretive assault on the scapegoating dynamic seemed doomed. Instead, we decided to work indirectly to weaken the collective need for fragmentation which underlay the continual transformation of leader into scapegoat. We outlined possible targets for this effort: developing staff skills and organization-wide esprit through in-house and external educational interventions; formulating new hiring policies which would seek out individuals committed to strengthening the organization at its center; restructuring the organization in ways that took into account the need for some functional separations of dissident subgroups but also emphasized new tasks and systems which united and integrated these subgroups (that is, projects which required nationality and language integration). We wanted to recognize the implications of the profound intergroup differences present in the staff, and we also agreed to add connecting elements which would decrease the threat of increasing integration. In essence, M. and I filtered all organizational change through the idea of weakening the collective scapegoating dynamic.

Five years earlier, M. had shown that he had the courage to risk saying the unsayable; now he also had the position of leadership to effect organizational change in a patient and noninflammatory fashion. He understood that staying in his job almost certainly required these changes and, unlike his many predecessors, he had the advantage of a concept to explain the leadership-scapegoating behavior and a consultant who would work beside him and support him. This last element turned out to be critical—and not just because of the information and perspective I could provide. Something more insidious happened which was to remake our consultation in an unexpected way.

M. and I met in my spacious office in Sausalito, an affluent suburb near San Francisco. In contrast, M.'s organization was located in a poverty area; its offices were plain and cramped. My consultation fee was high compared to the salaries of him and his staff as well as the salaries of most of the organization's clients. The staff was aware of these fiduciary contrasts; on occasion, we had held retreats in my offices. At these times, although I was treated with great deference, there were always veiled references to luxury, money, status, and racial differences between the consultant and the organization's staff.

From time to time, I felt vaguely uncomfortable about these fee and space arrangements. However, I did not decrease my fee or hold down regular increases. On three occasions in the five years of consultation, I insisted on coming to the agency site itself to see the staff in their own habitat. Twice the appointment was canceled and the third time much of the staff was mysteriously absent. I was also never able to attend the banquets, fund raisers, or other organizational events that have been used to celebrate its growth and success. Perhaps most important, I continued to be always the only ethnic outsider employed by the organization.

In the course of several years, it became clear to M. and me that part of the reason for the success of our work together and its effects on his tenure as leader was the way we, as a consultant pair, had become the new scapegoat for the increasingly successful organization. Despite our gradual changes in personnel and structure, the interethnic antagonisms continued to be fierce, even escalating, fueled by worsening international relations. Nor

115

had there been internal "insight" work within the organization that might have buffered this ever-present disruptive dynamic. The scapegoat was still an essential requirement for this organization to cohere, much as the scapegoat child had been an essential requirement of life in Le Guin's Omelas. In effect, the staff group accepted M.'s leadership even when his policies moved the organization toward integration of differences, but they did this by projecting their negative feelings onto the "outside" consultant and the consulting relationship. Together we were viewed as a leadership unit split into good and bad. He was the brilliant, rational, risk-taking hero while I was the dark, mysterious, greedy, shadowy overlord—the white devil, as M. once heard a person refer to me in the bathroom. M. was viewed as being strong enough to handle my potentially corrupting influence; his ability to do so probably added to his charisma. With M.'s tacit support, I established the valence for my "enemy status" quite unwittingly through choice of site, money arrangements, the secrecy of our work, my isolation from others, and the lack of other Caucasians in the situation.

In this organization, the pressure to find a victim had not altered, but the identity of the victim had changed. The consultancy process had become a scapegoat-in-the-mind for staff, much as fired leaders and institutional chaos had been the scapegoat-in-fact five years before.

How should we assess such an outcome in this consultancy process? The transfer of the negative projections away from the leader onto the consultant had allowed M. to survive as he carried out policies of integration. Without the consultancy as lightning rod, his job would have been continually in jeopardy. On the surface, at least, it is difficult to see harm in such an arrangement as long as the organization and its leader are thriving. Negative projections onto the consultant is as integral to the consultant's role as negative transference is to therapists.

Furthermore, in assessing damage to individuals or a social system, it is important to distinguish between the scapegoat-in-the-mind and the scapegoat-in-fact. The consultancy changed the situation so that it resembled a family or island group, where the victim of the scapegoating dynamic is more "incast" than outcast. Families rarely expel their problems: the prodigal son is allowed to return, as are other black sheep or victims, because they are needed to maintain the psychological equilibrium as well as to fill other family roles and functions. There was no overt damage to me or to M. as there had been to the five fired leaders before him. On the contrary, as individuals each of us gained greatly from the consultation process, and the organization benefited from the improved leadership skills of its director.

But there were costs that are not obvious. There was considerable cost to M., who learned little about dealing with the negative side of the authority vested in his role and so may not have been fully creative in his leadership. There was a similar creative cost to the organization as a whole and to some subgroups by continuing to deal through mechanisms of projection rather than exploration. In fact, M. had consulted with me about the way several of his best staff, outspoken and risk-taking individuals, were isolated and ostracized when they offered ideas and programs that required interethnic group cooperation. Scapegoating of whatever kind is never without cost. The effect of leaving out any element of a system always has repercussions in parallel process throughout the rest of the system. Here, M. felt muzzled, and his best personnel were constrained from acting in venturesome ways. Moreover, the consultancy, while serving a "helpful" symbolic function as alter-scapegoat, was thereby limited in providing information or interpretations that could have been well used by the organization.

Perhaps this arrangement was the most that could be attempted with such an embattled organization. These and other costs may seem part and parcel of my role and small compared to providing a vessel to contain the chaos and destructiveness that existed before M., the organization, and I began our dance together. It is very hard to imagine not having a scapegoat in this tension-filled system. Situations like the utopia of Omelas or this consultation always depend on their scapegoat, just as the ideal vision of a perfected man or woman depends on the projected shadow.

All organizational consultants who work in depth will inevitably be contaminated by the scapegoat archetype. No matter how carefully they work and at what pace, they are outsiders who say the unsayable, who speak the truth. They shame those who know; they anger those who don't. They are like the proverbial messengers who bring bad news and are punished for it.

117

Even if their work and information improves the situation, their presence is an embarrassment. Consultants need to contain this group anger, usually at some personal and professional cost. This may mean limiting what they will accept as their goals. It also means making peace with their liminality in the system in much the same way most therapists accept theirs. Negative as well as positive transference in organizational consultation comes with the work, and consultants can abuse organizations by emphasizing the positive and using it to their own advantage. The familiar transformation of high-level consultant to CEO is an outcome similar to a therapist sleeping with an analysand. It feels good at the time, but it rarely works out.

Unfortunately, once M. and I had uncovered and analyzed the scapegoat role the consultancy was inadvertently playing in the organization, the consultation itself was altered and could not go on as before. New insights create new dynamics which create new insights. The next step in an organization's development process often rides on what is done with this expanding awareness; when critical organizational insights can find no new mechanism of expression, development stagnates.

In this case, the risk focused on M. and his role. What M. knew about the consultation (which he valued a great deal) became more and more frustrating to him personally and stultifying to his leadership role. M. began to complain to me of a lack of challenge in his job; he felt less creative as a leader and less creative as a man. He became more aware of the degree of stagnation that was accepted by his staff in their programs, their unwillingness to take chances and risk change. M. now felt he should have brought the issue of the scapegoating dynamic back to the staff at various times in the past, but he was unwilling or unable to take the risk now. He was afraid of reversion to the too-familiar "kill the leader" posture. He did not want to endanger the organization's progress or risk his future career. And he was no longer the rebellious student hero. He talked about his new child and the house he planned to buy in a prestigious neighborhood. Perhaps he had reached his own personal limit as a leader in this phase of his life, but he was unable to face his limitations in our weekly conversations. Eventually, he accepted an offer to leave his position for another leadership job with better pay and a less volatile staff group. The organization hired his assistant to take his place; she was far less able than he, but also less threatening as an agent of change. I was not asked to continue my consultation.

In individual work, the shadow, including that part of the shadow constellated by the scapegoat, must be integrated by the person or individuation will be limited. So, too, with collective work. Development of a collective requires a willingness to take responsibility for exploring the meanings of its collective shadow—its scapegoats and scapegoating process. A mechanism must be established to minimize and interpret the individual and collective shadow projections that feed the scapegoating process. M. and I took the first steps to contain what had been a profoundly dysfunctional pattern of scapegoating all leadership. But the interpreter function, a mechanism for speaking the truth about the intergroup rivalries and their effect on the organization, was never adequately developed. Despite M.'s leadership position, the consultancy did not really alter the intergroup scapegoating dynamic that had destroyed five past leaders. The first part of the consultation clarified the problem and also readied the organization for change through education and restructuring. But the insight function remained split off, imparted to me and M.; it never penetrated into his staff, the board of directors, the secretaries. Organizations often hire their consultants as leaders in order to take this next step. Others find a person or persons—the internal interpreter—to continue this vital work. M.'s organization may yet take this step, but it had not done so when he and I left.

In individual analytic work, the most personally meaningful and conflicting parts of the psyche are projected into the analytic container to be worked on and, when possible, transformed. The analyst's office, his or her personage, and the dyadic amalgam are gradually brought into the psyche of the patient and transformed into figures which have archetypal and personal meaning. These figures, such as wise old man, witch, shaman, totem animal, or well-remembered family member or teacher, present themselves in dreams, fantasy, and imagination and may be called forth at critical times for conscious and unconscious internal dialogue. In organizational consultation, a similar internalization of the process occurs and may lead to a person or subgroup within the organization taking up the consultative function. Sometimes it is a wise and experienced person who is outside the chain of command and who becomes an informal advisor to the chief executive; or the staff may use one department or another to provide internal consultation; or management may learn to use periodic retreats to move deeper into their creative process. Formal consultation externalizes this meaning-generating function at those times when the organization needs to give it special prominence—especially in times of transition and crisis, when the organization can no longer manage its internal differences. An organization under stress which develops a pattern of excluding and denying its dissident elements rather than including them as part of its developmental process may need an outsider to loosen the boundaries and provide face-saving potential. But eventually the consultative function, with knowledge of scapegoats and scapegoating, must be reabsorbed into the body of the organization and must continue to be used.

Partially as a result of my experience with M.'s organization, I have made it a priority in my work with organizations to try to develop this internal interpreter function as the consultation unfolds. A first step is to develop a consultation relationship with the organization which models the kind of internal work required of its members and the organization as a whole. Working with important groups within the organization rather than just with the leader or other key personnel is particularly helpful. It is surprising how often an interpreter emerges from out of the membership, someone like M. in the situation above, who is able to speak from a perspective of the collective. I try to facilitate this development by providing education about unconscious collective process as a regular part of my work with an organization, including referring leadership and other interested subgroups or members to workshops and readings on this subject. The goal is to build a culture which awakens consciousness and values exploration and inquiry into its own processes.

It is my impression that depth consultation—consultation which deals with development through exploration of unconscious collective processes—is becoming more and more acceptable to modern organizations struggling to deal with greater diversity, complexity, and a more competitive marketplace. I recently took part in planning sessions for leadership training programs in California in which the reality of ethnic diversity is the main concern (it is projected that by the year two thousand, the number of whites will equal the number of Asians, Latinos, and Blacks). Most of the consultants and trainers present believed that anything less than providing upcoming leadership with tools that can be used to move toward transcending differences; holding opposites and polarities; and dealing with group, intergroup, and interethnic processes in depth would not be useful in dealing with the new multicentered, multiethnic California. In a similar vein, many professional and business gatherings are asking for process facilitation as part of their development programs.

Just prior to the breakup of the Soviet Union, Dr. Montero and I were asked by a member of the Senate to provide consultation to a conference in which there were to be high-level representatives from political, professional, and artistic groups in the United States and the Soviet Union. The group was to work together for a week in a relatively isolated setting, and there was prior experience of group struggles within and between the two subgroups which had subverted positive interactions. The Senate organizers had information that the Soviet delegation, which was made up of Lithuanians and Armenians as well as Russians, were dangerously hostile to one another, a fact which became a political reality within a year after the conference was held. Because of the explosive potential inherent in the gathering, we decided to provide an informal, voluntary "event" at the end of the day during which group issues, at the deepest level possible, could be discussed by whoever was interested. The event began slowly, but by the end of the week it was very well attended, and despite a great deal of realistic suspicion about who was keeping track of the proceedings and how it would be used by the respective governments, a fascinating and often profound discussion evolved, which included an appreciation of unconscious and collective forces driving the group. A great deal was learned which had the dual effect of making the conference more interesting for the participants and presaging the upcoming political events. That the method was at least acceptable is borne out by a later invitation to consult to a follow-up conference outside Moscow using a similar model, except that now the consultation was a formal part of the program. (This event, modified significantly by the timing of the conference—it took place during the aborted coup d'etat in August 1991—was referred to in Montero's foreword to this volume.)

Most interesting to me was the acceptance of this depth process model by governmental institutions and powerful individuals. Many political leaders now realize that complexity, diversity, and the greater risks of war increase the risks of ignoring or excluding any nation in the international collective. Perhaps soon they, too, will be more willing to accept a broader definition of consultation than simply providing facts and tactics. It is possible that in the near future political bodies will want access to their unconscious collective as part of their decision-making process, if we can learn to provide it.

Despite these hints of new developments, most organizations in trouble are still unwilling to undertake a depth exploration of the difficulties. Usually, rather than deal with potentially explosive conflicts and complexes, organizations resort even more readily than individuals to exporting their problems through firings, mergers, splits, and other structural changes which deny and obfuscate threatening shadow processes at work. Consultation, when allowed, is usually more like behavioral therapy than analysis. Strangely, "psychological" organizations—that is, mental health clinics and therapy training institutes which focus on individual development—are often less willing to accept consultation when they are in trouble than organizations such as businesses which are ostensibly less psychologically oriented. Perhaps the former are more aware of the danger of unconscious life. Receiving help requires the same humility and acceptance of woundedness as giving help. Organizations that are afraid to receive help, to learn about themselves in all their parts— including those parts that are excluded and victimized—are in trouble, just as individuals with the same constrictions in sharing and receiving help are in trouble. In my experience, *outside* consultation is usually the best way to begin exploring the collective roots of systemic problems in organizations. However, organizations can be remarkably self-protective, even when their competence or survival is at stake. After all, wars have been fought rather than submitting to the scrutiny of an outsider. So alternative internal approaches must be tried when resistance is too great.

If one is part of a collective that scapegoats and is afraid to look for help outside itself, learning more about collective process in general may be of some help. In such cultures of denial, and this can occur in even the most enlightened collection of individuals, members can also try to develop self-study groups, internal interpretive systems whose input may be less threatening than an outside voice. This difficult process is analogous perhaps to the kind of self-analysis that both Freud and Jung carried out on themselves (with such mixed results).

One organization that I belong to has been beset by scapegoating issues since its formation. Most members appreciate the problem but for reasons of unity and self-protection are afraid to bring in an outsider to help explore the issues. In this context, some of us have begun two projects with the long-term goal of increasing the developmental potential in the collective.

First, and least threatening, we created an internal publication, called *Connected Works,* whose editorial policy is to accept all contributions from members with minimal editing. These "individual contributions" are then conceptualized as "collective associations" about the organization as a whole. Much can be learned from such a projective instrument. For example, one of the most important regular contributors has remained anonymous despite the fact that our organization prides itself on openness and taking personal responsibility for behavior. There was a move within the membership to stop "anonymous" contributions, as if one could erase the condition which makes signed contributions too dangerous. By holding to the editorial policy, an interpretation to the collective was effectively made. The membership was forced to confront the anonymous interpreter figure and ponder our censorship of "truth speaking" and tolerance of scapegoating as a way to solve our collective difficulties.

Connected Works functions pragmatically as a listening and communication post for the membership. But it is also an interpreter of the unconscious collective process of our organization. It is always a constant source of amazement to the editorial board how individual contributions are also group utterances, how contributions fit together, how common themes develop unbidden which reflect the organizational unconscious and the collective mind.

We have built on this process by forming an organization-wide study group whose task is the study the collective unconscious of our organization. This more direct approach to our collective problems is far more controversial and threatening than the publication, although in form it is similar to other internal learning structures, such as "corporate universities" which function as internal consultants to their own parent organizations (Hampden-Turner 1990; Senge 1990). Just the presence of such structures has a potent impact on a community. In my organization, the study group challenges the entire membership to give more than lip service to the concept of a collective unconscious, which it espouses as something in which we all take part—not some "mystical" synchronistic entity beyond our ken but a flesh-and-blood unit with coherence and identity. The study group has had to develop a language and an analytic method to explore specific events as manifestations of this unconscious collective. We have begun by looking to our myths of origin, our group dreams and fantasies, as well as our internal process as a manifestation of the larger collective we represent and mirror. As might be expected, there have been some attempts by the organization to "sabotage" the group's work through unconscious scheduling slips and other classic resistances. However, thus far there is also a great deal of general support and interest in developing a richer perspective on who we are to each other and what we are enacting in and for the larger collective. It is too early to know how well these "experiments in progress" will serve organizations and whether they will develop in other organizations as an alternative to the more threatening "outsider" aspects of a consultant. It is clear that they serve a function different from the usual problem-solving committees, task forces, and the like because they are committed to exploration and a search for meaning in collective behavior rather than being geared to improvements and solutions.

Most recently, my colleagues and I have begun experimenting with groups which go a step beyond these in-house projects. Our interest continues to be in studying the process, potential, and limits of group development. One group we have begun has the conscious purpose of individuating through learning more about accessing our group's collective unconscious, its "other world" while being mindful of dynamic and archetypal processes such as scapegoating which limit and divert. We have called this group the *Face of God* group, emphasizing that God may see his "goal" in the face of the group as well as the individual. By design our "face" is as representative as possible—diverse in many

124

dimensions, such as age, race, and sexual orientation. What we share is an interest in unconscious group process and the way the Self manifests in groups. This group differs from self-study groups in that we focus on analytic investigation of process through our commitment to group individuation and spiritual development and our use of a variety of techniques which provide a doorway to our group consciousness. It differs from new-age ceremonial and celebrational groups because we study our group process, including the authority issues that so often plague spiritually minded groups and religious traditions.

The task of the group is as different as we imagined. There is an initial need for moving inward to explore and play and discover who we were, are, and might become and an equal force directed toward the outside to define ourselves by our instrumental abilities as a team. As with most individuals faced with the same task and dilemma, in the beginning the inward direction seemed most important—the development of safe and meaningful rituals for invoking the Self, for finding visionary elements in our group, for learning about individual linkages to our collective experience. But that inward direction also brought out our psychological and subgroup differences, and the psychological task of integrating diversity without erasing difference proved enormous. Meditating, drumming, or chanting together could be profound, and it could also be a way of turning away from stereotyping behaviors such as racism and sexism as well as anger, hostility, and sexual attractions which lay just below the surface. It is no wonder that spiritual institutions are so cult-like; it is far easier to accept and depend on charismatic leadership and ecstatic techniques than to work out group issues that might undermine cohesion. But we have also found that working on psychological process could become an addictive cul-de-sac which inhibited the group's spiritual development and a closer relationship with the group self. Learning how to maintain a balance between psychological and spiritual exploration, between evoking and monitoring process and the developing group self, has grown with time and trust. Perhaps that is at the heart of the group individuation process itself. But mindful of Jung's dictum to "create equivalent value," we are also beginning to work towards bringing some of the fruits of our experiment back into the larger

125

community without diverting or losing what we have already gained on our Island.

I am hopeful that we are not idiosyncratic in our interest but part of a collective movement in which new forms of a renewed commitment to the psychological development of the collective, its "individuation," for surely that is one area where our individual futures as members of the human collective and the planet's collective must lie. Perhaps it is in that commitment to help others, valuing others who share our cosmic home as much as our selves, that Jung's concept of "equivalent value" will find its greatest meaning.

Notes

Chapter 1

1. Sylvia Perera's book on the scapegoat (1986) is an excellent source for historical evidence and examples.

2. The name Omelas, as Le Guin informs us, does not have some mystical meaning. It is simply a town, Salem, in Oregon near where Le Guin lives, spelled backward. Salem, of course, is also the name of the site of the famous Massachusetts witch trials, which have a parallel in her story.

3. Henderson (1991) has also called attention to this lack of an effective social attitude within Jungian circles.

Chapter 3

4. A personal communication with A. Guggenbühl-Craig, 1991.

5. If not confidential, it would be fascinating to explore the specific machinations of power that move a scientific community in our times, a sort of fifty-year update on what C. P. Snow (1937) documented so well in his series of novels about the scientific academy in England during the development of the atomic bomb.

6. See Henderson (1967) and van Gennep (1960) for classic discussions of the role of groups in initiation.

Chapter 5

7. For example, the incredible advances in the world communications net have created whole new ways of collective thinking and experiencing. Less dramatic but also important are the experimental methods of studying unconscious progress in small and large groups, such as promulgated by group relations conferences, and their impact on business and government structures and policy (Colman and Bexton 1975; Colman and Geller 1985).

Chapter 6

8. The paradoxical use of "individuation" to describe a collective process is at the heart of the rest of this chapter.

Bibliography

Berne, E. 1964. *Games People Play: The Psychology of Human Relationships.* New York: Grove Press.

Berry, T. 1988. *The Dream of the Earth.* San Francisco: Sierra Books.

Bion, W. R. 1959. *Experiences in Groups.* New York: Basic Books. (Also 1974. New York: Ballantine Books.)

Burkhardt, Jacob. 1929. *The Civilization of the Renaissance in Italy.* New York: Harper and Row.

Christensen, W. 1989. A fashion for ecstacy: Ancient Mayan body modifications. *Modern Primitives.* San Francisco: Re/search Publications.

Colman, A. D. 1989. The scapegoat: A psychological perspective. *Contributions to Social and Political Science,* F. Gabelnick and A. W. Carr, eds. Washington, D.C.: A. K. Rice Institute.

Colman, A. D., and H. Bexton, eds. 1975. *Group Relations Reader I.* Washington, D.C.: A. K. Rice Institute.

Colman, A. D., and L. L. Colman. 1975. *Love and Ecstasy.* New York: Seabury.

Colman, A. D., and M. Geller, eds. 1985. *Group Relations Reader II.* Washington, D.C.: A. K. Rice Institute.

Colman, A. D., and P. Montero. 1989. Archetypes of group process. San Francisco: C. G. Jung Institute.

Corbin, H. 1975. The *imago templi* and secular norms. *Spring,* pp. 163–185.

Deikman, A. 1990. *The Wrong Way Home: Uncovering Patterns of Cult Behavior in American Society.* Boston: Beacon Press.

Dostoyevsky, F. 1879. *The Brothers Karamazov.* New York: Random House.

Eliade, Mircea. 1964. *Shamanism: Archaic Techniques of Ecstasy.* Princeton, N.J.: Princeton University Press.

Erickson, E. 1972. Play and actuality. *Play and Development,* Marin W. Piers, ed. New York: Norton.

Fordham, M. 1985. *Explorations into the Self.* London: Academic Press.

―――――. 1993. Notes for the formation of a model of infant development. *Journal of Analytical Psychology.* 38:5–12.

Freud, S. 1921. Group psychology and the analysis of the ego. *SE,* vol 18. London: Hogarth Press, 1955.

―――――. 1930. *Civilization and Its Discontents. SE,* vol. 21. London: Hogarth Press, 1953.

Friedan, B. 1963. *The Feminine Mystique.* New York: Norton.

Gibbard, G. S., J. J. Hartman, and R. D. Mann, eds. 1974. Introduction to section II: Group process and development. *Analysis in Groups.* San Francisco: Jossey-Bass.

Girard, Rene. 1987. Generative scapegoating. *Violent Origins: Ritual Killing and Cultural Formation,* Robert G. Hamerton-Kelly, ed. Stanford, Calif.: Stanford University Press.

Golding, W. 1958. *Lord of the Flies.* London: Faber and Faber.

Hampden-Turner, C. 1990. *Charting the Corporate Mind: Graphic Solutions to Business Conflicts.* New York: Free Press.

Hannah, Barbara. 1976. *Jung: His Life and Work, A Biographical Memoir.* New York: Putnam.

Harner, M. 1982. *The Way of the Shaman.* New York: Bantam.

Henderson, J. 1967. *Thresholds of Initiation.* Middletown, Conn.: Wesleyan University Press.

―――――. 1991. C. G. Jung's psychology: Additions and extensions. *Journal of Analytical Psychology* 36:429–442.

Herschell, A. J. 1962. *The Prophets.* New York: Harper and Row.

Hillis, R. E. 1985. Psyche and annihilation. *Psychological Perspectives* 16:51–73.

Hultkrantz, A. A. 1973. Definition of shamanism. *Temenos* 9:25–37.

Jackson, D. D. 1960. Introduction. *Etiology of Schizophrenia,* D. D. Jackson, ed. New York: Basic Books.

Jackson, S. 1975. The lottery. *Classic Short Stories.* New York: Creative Education.

Jacob, D. 1987. *The Brutality of Nations.* New York: Knopf.

Janis, I. L. 1950. Psychological stress. *Psychoanalytic and Behavioral Studies of Surgical Patients.* London: Chapman and Hall.

Joffe, W. G., and Sandler, J. 1965. Notes on pain, depression and individuation. *Psychoanalytic Study of the Child* 20:394–424.

Jones, Maxwell. 1953. *The Therapeutic Community.* New York: Basic Books.

Jung, C. G. 1916. Adaptation, individuation, collectivity. In *CW* 18:449–454. Princeton, N.J.: Princeton University Press, 1973.

―――――. 1921. *Psychological Types. CW,* vol. 6. Princeton, N.J.: Princeton University Press, 1971.

_____. 1943. On the psychology of the unconscious. In *CW* 7:3–121. Princeton, N.J.: Princeton University Press, 1953, 1966.

_____. 1948. The phenomenology of the spirit in fairytales. In *CW* 9i:207–254. Princeton, N.J.: Princeton University Press, 1959.

_____. 1950. Concerning rebirth. In *CW* 9i:113–147. Princeton, N.J.: Princeton University Press, 1959.

_____. 1952. *Symbols of Transformation. CW*, vol. 5. Princeton, N.J.: Princeton University Press, 1956.

_____. 1957. The undiscovered self (present and future). In *CW* 10:245–304. Princeton, N.J.: Princeton University Press, 1964.

_____. 1958. Flying saucers: A modern myth of things seen in the skies. In *CW* 10:307–434. Princeton, N.J.: Princeton University Press, 1970.

_____. 1965. *Memories, Dreams, Reflections*. New York: Vintage.

Klein, M. 1959. Our adult world and its roots in infancy. *Human Relations* 12:291–303.

Le Guin, U. K. 1975. The ones who walk away from Omelas. *The Wind's Twelve Quarters*. New York: Harper.

Lessing, D. 1988. *The Fifth Child*. New York: Random House.

Lifton, R. J. 1964. On death and death symbolism: The Hiroshima disaster. *Psychiatry* 27:191–210.

Llosa, Mario Vargas. 1990. Questions of conquest: What Columbus wrought, and what he did not. *Harper's* (December), pp. 45–53.

Machiavelli, Niccolò. 1950. *The Prince*. New York: Random House.

Mahler, M. S. 1972. On the first three subphases of the separation-individuation process. *International Journal of Psychoanalysis* 53:333–338.

Maidenbaum, Aryeh, and Stephen A., Martin, eds. 1991. *Lingering Shadows: Jungians, Freudians, and Anti-Semitism*. Boston: Shambhala.

Mason, E., trans. 1976. *Arthurian Chronicles 1115*. New York: Dutton.

Matthews, J. 1989. *The Elements of the Arthurian Tradition*. Shaftesbury: Element.

Miller, E. J., and A. K. Rice. 1965. *Learning for Leadership*. London: Tavistock.

Mishima, Y. 1965. *The Sailor Who Fell from Grace with the Sea*. Trans. J. Nathan. New York: Vintage International.

Mitchell, S., trans. 1988. *Tao Te Ching*. New York: Harper and Row.

Montero, P. 1992. The imaginal at crossings: A soul's view of organizational and individual analysis. *Gender and Soul in Psychotherapy*, N. Schwartz-Salant and M. Stein, eds. Wilmette, Ill.: Chiron Publications.

Naifeh, S. 1993. Experiencing the Self. *The San Francisco Jung Institute Library Journal* 12:5–27.

Pearce, C. P. 1973. *The Crack in the Cosmic Egg.* New York: Pocket Books.

Perera, S. B. 1986. *The Scapegoat Complex.* Toronto: Inner City Books.

Perls, F., R. F. Hefferline, and P. Goodman. 1951. *Gestalt Therapy: Excitement and Growth in Human Personality.* New York: Julian Press.

Perry, J. W. 1987. *The Heart of History.* Albany, N.Y.: State University of New York Press.

Renault, Mary. 1958. *The King Must Die.* New York: Random House.

Rioch, David. 1971. Foreword. A. D. Colman, *The Planned Environment in Psychiatric Treatment.* Springfield, Ill: Thomas, 1971.

Russell, Jeffrey Burton. 1988. The evil one. *Facing Evil: Light at the Core of Darkness,* ed. H. A. Wilmer. La Salle, Ill.: Open Court.

Samuels, Andrew. 1992. National psychology, national socialism, and analytical psychology: Reflections on Jung and anti-Semitism. Part I. *Journal of Analytical Psychology* 37:3–28.

Sapir, E. 1949. *Selected Writing of Edward Sapir in Language, Culture, and Personality.* David G. Mandelbaum, ed. Berkeley, Calif.: University of California Press.

Satir, Virginia. 1967. *Conjoint Family Therapy.* Palo Alto, Calif.: Science and Behavior Books.

Schell, J. 1982. *The Fate of the Earth.* New York: Knopf.

Senge, P. M. 1990. *The Fifth Discipline: The Art and Practice of the Learning Organization.* New York: Doubleday.

Snow, C. P. 1985. *Strangers and Brothers.* New York: Scribner.

Spiegelman, J. M. 1988. *Jungian Analysts: Their Visions and Vulnerabilities.* Scottsdale, Ariz.: New Falcon Press.

Stein, M., and J. Hollwitz, eds. 1992. *Psyche at Work: Workplace Applications of Jungian Analytical Psychology.* Wilmette, Ill.: Chiron Publications.

van Gennep, Arnold. 1960. *Rites of Passage.* Chicago: University of Chicago Press.

Wilmer, H. A. 1958. *Social Psychiatry in Action: A Therapeutic Community.* Springfield, Ill.: Thomas.

Winnicott, D. W. 1953. Transitional objects and transitional phenomena. *International Journal of Psychoanalysis* 24:89–97.

Index

Myth
  community embodying, 79
  group as embodying, 80–83
  and story as language of the
    group's collective
    unconscious, 78
Myth of origin, 102–3

N

Narcissistic individualism, 32
Notes, 127–28

O

Oedipus Rex, Freud's great collective
  myth as, 80
Omelas
  as essential requirement of life,
    116, 117
  origin of name of, 127
  paradise metaphor of miserable
    child for, 10–13
  walkaways from, 15
Organizational self, 100

P

Pairing in Bion's theory of group
  behavior, 23
Patterns of behavior
  roots in the collective
    unconscious of, 103
  transforming acts into, 77
Perera, Sylvia, 127
Perry, John, 4
Pizarro, Francisco, 41
Platonic tradition of analytical
  psychology, x
Political science as dealing with the
  psychology of the collective, 99
Political systems, 91–92
Primordial image (archetype), 88–89
Projections onto the consultant,
  negative, 116–17
Prophets, personal lives given up for
  collective ones by, 62
Puer archetype, 46

R

Rainmaker, Jung's story of, 49–50
Reintegration, 27
  precipitating, 37
Religious experiences, ecstatic, 35
Renault, Mary, 91
Rice, Ken, as cocreator of group
  relations theory, *xvii*
Rioch, David, *xvii*
  connection between war and
    unconscious group process
    for, *xix*
Rites of initiation, 98
Round Table, myths of King Arthur's,
  79–80, 84–86, 93
Russell, Jeffrey Burton, 56
Russia, demise of communism in,
  xi–xii

S

Savio, Mario, 17–18
Scapegoat
  Aaron as, 7, 8
  boundary between group
    members and, 9
  as carrying an organization's
    development potential,
    109–10
  as central group myth, 80–81
  colleague at Jungian institute as,
    2
  defined, 6
  denying the humanity of, 112–13
  as holding the hidden
    corruption and pain, 104, 112
  Jesus as, 8, 14, 16–17, 80
  Jung's concept of individuation
    and, 1–20
  in literature, 8
  modern examples of the ethnic,
    9
  as part of organization's
    troubled process and not the
    cause, 106
  transformation into savior of,
    16–17

Index

139